The Secrets to Breaking Soul Ties

A Guide to Freedom from Toxic Relationships

Pamela Wilson

© 2017 Pamela Wilson
All rights reserved.

ISBN: 1978110847
ISBN 13: 9781978110847

Dedication

*All praise to Jesus who gave me the revelation, wisdom
and inspiration to write this book.
To my mom for recognizing and encouraging my writing gift.
To all of the women who have settled for less.*

Acknowledgements

To Jen, thank you for sacrificing your time to give me honest feedback about this book.

To Uncle for always seeing the good in me and encouraging me to soar above obstacles.

To Pop Williams for your beautiful smile and peaceful nature.

To every one who prayed over the manuscript, encouraged me to finish, offered feedback and spoke kind words.

Table Of Contents

Acknowledgements		v
Introduction		ix
1	Lies We Tell Ourselves	1
2	Signs of a Toxic Relationship/Soul Tie	8
3	What is a Soul Tie?	17
4	Comfortable with Crazy	25
5	Seducing Spirits	30
6	Man Traps	47
7	The Masquerade	52
8	Red Flags	59
9	Why You Chose Him	73
10	Still Broken	87
11	The Aftermath of Soul Ties	91
12	Reality Check	99
13	Know Your Worth	109
14	Guard Your Heart	113
15	God's Restoration	126
16	Be Free	131
Appendix		149

Introduction

ARE YOU IN a crazy relationship? Have you settled for a man who only meets half of your needs, half of the time or not at all? If you answered yes to either of these questions, "Congratulations!" You just took a bold step in the right direction. The first step in solving a problem is in recognizing that you have one. So get comfortable, go to your favorite spot and read on to discover how you got into this chaos.

If you're like me, you've looked back on some of your relationships and wondered, "What was I thinking?" It's like my brain went on vacation. What I didn't know at the time was that there was something broken in me. I was always trying to fix a guy as if he was a science project that I could put together. In other cases, the guy that I was interested in took the lead role in trying to play me like an instrument. In all fairness, there are men who wreak havoc in your life, but they don't do it on purpose. They're just broken in spirit. On the other hand, there are perpetrators whose main objective is to manipulate you for their gain. These counterfeit suitors are very clever and they are excellent actors, but don't feel bad if you've been duped into "fix-him-up" projects or if you have wasted time dating wolves in sheep's clothing. You are not alone and there is help for you.

I eventually realized that a broken man needs Jesus and so does a broken woman. A man has to face his shortcomings just like I had to face mine. It is not my job to become his savior. I learned that the way you begin a relationship is usually how it will end. For instance, if you begin a relationship like you're his mother, you'll probably have to assume that role for the duration of the relationship unless there is divine intervention.

As we set out on this journey to freedom, there may be strong doses of truth on the pages of this book and I hope that you receive it. Truth is like brussel sprouts and cod liver oil. We may not like the taste, but there is great benefit to be gained. I invite you to pledge to face the truth even when you're tempted to deny it. Besides, the alternative is unattractive – ignoring the truth and continuing to suffer from a broken heart. I had to face the same truths that I'm sharing with you in this book and my life is better because of it. Now that you have committed to facing the truth, let's get back to our discussion.

Maybe you are in a toxic relationship because you believe that half of a man is better than no man. Perhaps, unhealthy relationships were modeled in your family or community so you never really expect much from a man. Maybe you don't feel worthy of respect and genuine love because of insecurity, abuse, rejection, abandonment or betrayal. Or maybe as you grew older you accepted the lie that half a man is better than no man. Whatever the reason, you can break the cycle of deceit and heartache. To sum it up, you and I can both admit that we've been involved in less than desirable relationships. So, what's next?

The first thing you need to do is take inventory of yourself. What kind of man do you repeatedly attract or find yourself drawn to? Are they smooth talkers with no substance? Tall and athletic with no integrity? Are they "mama's boys" who value their mothers' opinion more than yours? Does it seem like there's a sign on your forehead that reads, "Send me all of the broken, irresponsible, immature, lying, non-committal men?" There's a reason that you attract the same type of guy. Uncovering that reason requires some soul-searching, which is why I need you to take your time in answering the next set of questions. What areas of your life need to be repaired, healed or restored? Do you confuse lust with love? Are you hurt because your parent, another relative or ex-boyfriend rejected, abandoned or abused you? Are you bitter about your childhood, teenage years or adulthood? Would you say that you know your purpose for living? These are serious questions that deserve sincere answers. IF you want to be free from toxic decisions, you have to be honest with yourself. Other than God, no one knows you better than yourself. Only when you face the truth can you begin to live the life that God intended.

I spend years skating around the truth, blaming others and ignoring the root of my problem. In the bible, God refers to believers as trees (Psalm 1:3), but if a tree develops a fungus, the gardener has to investigate the root cause of the deadly bacteria and cut off its supply. Here is one of the biggest secrets that changed my life. One day I prayed and asked my heavenly Father, "What is at the root of my failures?" " Why do I keep attracting the same type of guy? The source of my failure and poor-decision making was rooted in rejection and abandonment expressed through unforgiveness, bitterness and denial. These spirits are silent killers. They steal your joy, peace and love. These spiritual bacteria happily grown in the soil of your heart hoping to poison every aspect of your life.

Ask the Holy Spirit this question: "Why have my relationships ended in failure?" Wait for an answer and jot it down. The Holy Spirit will lead and guide you into all truth (John 16:13). You may need to keep a small notepad with you. More revelation may come while you're driving, washing dishes, showering, cooking, attending church, watching television or conversing with a friend. God may take you back to your high school years. Remember, who you are at this present moment is a composite of generational, societal, cultural and unseen influences known as "works of the flesh" (Gal. 5:19-21) and evil spirits (Eph. 6:11-12). Some belief systems were passed down from your great-grandparents while other philosophies were shaped by television, celebrities and social media. In some families, cultural expectations inform and control a person's decisions. God loves desires for us to be truthful (Psalm 51:6). It is God's joy to see his daughters walking in truth; no longer bound or deceived.

The second thing you need to do before we go any further is swallow a strong pill of truth. I need you to admit that you *chose* to be with him. Take responsibility for your part in this fiasco. If your relationship is not the result of sexual abuse, an arranged marriage or kidnapping, no one forced you into a relationship with this man. Part of your healing will involve taking responsibility for your actions. You can't fix what you won't face. Now that we've established that fact, let's talk about the man's role in your current misery.

Typically, the man who is the source of your heartache fits one of two general profiles. He's usually "Mr. Rude" or "Mr. Perfect. Both kinds of men can possess the same characteristics. Either type can be ego maniacs, immature or unstable. Mr. Rude is usually emotionally unavailable while Mr. Perfect gives the appearance of being emotionally connected to you. Each type can be conceited and pretend that they're interested in you until they achieve a certain goal. What makes them different from each other is their presentation.

For instance, Sir Rudeness disappoints, dishonors, and lies to you over and over again and the crazy thing is that you accept his behavior. Nothing about him is gentle (unless it benefits him at the moment). You know the type: macho, quick-tempered, daredevil who will fight at the drop of a dime. He has no obvious fears or insecurities. He speaks his mind quite often and doesn't care who he offends including you. He is in love with himself and believes that he is always right.

Mr. Charming, on the other hand, says and does all the right things. He's sensitive and attentive to all of your needs, always knows what to say and do to make you feel better, but the knot in your stomach tells you that something isn't right.

And then there's the "Mystery Man". He's a little harder to peg. He's not rude, but he's not sensitive either. He's somewhere in the middle. You rarely know what he's thinking, but his aloof mannerisms intrigue you all the more. While Sir Rudeness and Mr. Charming can have a problem holding down a job, Mystery Man is definitely challenged in that department. Mystery Man also keeps you guessing, wondering if you've done enough. That's part of his charm and also part of his dysfunction. Whether you're dating Mr. Rude, Mr. Charming, Mystery Man, or a man who possesses a combination of each personality type, you know something is wrong. Nevertheless, you ignore your feelings and convince yourself that half a man is better than no man. Besides, no one is perfect. And the list of excuses goes on and on.

So you settle for a fraction of the joy that you deserve. You may even have slipped into an imaginary world where you pretend that he's better than he really is. Although you are dissatisfied with the relationship, it's like an invisible magnet keeps pulling you toward him. You know that you should break up with him, but you feel powerless. The relationship is weighing you down, but you hold on and hope for the best while his devilish, charming and confusing ways grip your soul. If these experiences describe your situation, you are in a soul tie.

Simply put, your soul is in prison. Your soul is tied to his soul, which is creating a negative impact on your life. In other words, your mind, emotions and will are tied to him like glue. Your thoughts, feelings, decisions, time and energy revolve around him. As the soul tie progresses, you lower your standards, compromise your values, or tolerate more disrespect than you could have ever imagined. You are unsure of his sincerity or fully aware of his insincerity. You begin to feel worthless, insecure, confused or crazy. You begin to view bad treatment or emotional unavailability as acceptable. Nervousness, anxiety, tension, fear, and restlessness become a part of your identity.

The Secrets to Breaking Soul Ties is designed to help you understand why you chose him, why it's been difficult to leave him and how to break free from the unhealthy relationship. All men aren't bad, but some men are bad for you. This book will help you identify the signs of a toxic relationship. It will also offer practical ways to guard your heart from "fix-him-up projects" and counterfeit suitors so you can live the life that God intended, celebrate yourself, and change the way you look at potential mates.

1
Lies We Tell Ourselves

Half of a Man Is Better Than No Man
SOME PEOPLE SAY that half a man is better than no man, but I strongly disagree with that statement. Would you go to a car dealership and buy half a car? Where would you go in a jalopy like that? Nowhere! And that's exactly where you will go with half of a man. He may not have a vision for his life and is unable or unwilling to encourage and strengthen you or he may have a vision for his life, but he is completely self-absorbed. His world begins and ends with himself. He may even brag about his sexual prowess, but what about his character?

Does he keep his promises or does he make commitments and break them? How does he respond in crises? Do you always have to rescue him? Is he still living with his momma? Does he have his own place or is he looking to move in with you? Does he have a job or career? Does he have the ability to build you up when you feel torn down? Is God the source of his decision-making or does he make decisions based on his feelings? Does he have an ongoing, growing, thriving relationship with the Lord or does he go to church to please you? Has he promised you that he will go to church with you after you marry him?

Maybe he's a little more slick. Perhaps, he goes to church, carries a bible and attends bible study, but his motives are impure. He knows what you like and he plays the game long enough to get what he wants. My sister, half of a man is not better than no man. You know the old saying, "I can do bad all by myself." Well, don't be bad to yourself, be good to yourself and please don't add "half-a-man" to your shopping list. It is ungodly and there is no scripture to support that product.

Adam was a mature man before God presented Eve to him. He was gainfully employed as the manager of the Garden of Eden. He named all of the animals, talked with God on a regular basis, and could hear, receive and obey the instructions that came from His heavenly Father. Adam was the first example of manhood and Jesus solidified that role through his sacrifice on the cross. A godly man will sacrifice himself for you (Eph. 5:25). He must also love God first and love himself before he can love you (Luke 10:27; Eph. 5:28). Ladies, ladies, ladies, half-a-man just won't do.

Still unconvinced? Try eating a half-baked cake or a half-baked chicken. It may look appetizing, but once you bite into it, you have to throw it in the garbage can. A half-baked man will yield the same results. Everything looks wonderful on the outside - great smile, nice body, and smooth words, but when you bite into his promises, all you get are half-truths, immaturity, shattered dreams and spiritual scar tissue. You want a whole man. Half-a-man won't do!

Men Will Be Men
It's okay if he runs around on me sometimes. After all, I can't expect him to be loyal to one woman. Lies! The devil is a liar! A man sent by God will be faithful to one woman just as Jesus Christ is faithful to His bride. Believers are the body of Christ and Jesus **never** cheats on her! He is loyal and promises to **never** leave us nor forsake us (Heb. 13:5). A real man will recognize the treasure that you are and he will be faithful to his "good thing" (Prov. 18:22).

I think we should change the statement from "men will be men" to "boys will be boys." It's boys who don't have the ability to remain faithful to one woman. It's boys who don't know how to grow in grace and in the knowledge of one woman. It is a boy who does not know how to bridle his passions. It is a boy who does not have the maturity, stability, or tenacity to commit to one woman. It is a boy who is unable to love and support one woman.

Men of God will be men of God. They will govern their lives by biblical principles. They will make decisions that line up with the word of God. They will not copy the behavior of the world. They will not sag their pants. They will treat you like a queen. They will honor you even in your absence because they are honorable. Men of God have integrity. Their actions match their words. They will not use flattery or trickery to lure you into a den of deceit. They will be selfless, preferring you over themselves. They will never dishonor your name or place you in compromising situations. They will always help you to maintain your purity (Eph. 5:26). They will not suggest that you watch pornography or engage in sex before marriage. They will keep their word and honor their commitments.

Do you have a boy or a man of God? How does he treat his mother, his sisters, his brothers? How does he treat strangers, cashiers, waitresses, people who can't do anything for him? A man of God will demonstrate the character of Christ. Manhood is not limited to an adult body and a driver's license. Evaluating the goodness of a man is much like inspecting a car. The car may look magnificent on the outside, but what's beneath the hood? What's under the hood is more valuable. Try driving a good-looking car that has no engine. You won't get very far. Try being with a handsome man who has a wicked heart. You won't get very far in that relationship without encountering bumps, bruises, potholes, major break-downs and malfunctions along the highway of that soul-damaging relationship. You don't want a boy in a man's body.

I Can Change Him
I've heard testimonies about women who prayed and fasted and their husbands became pastors and mighty men of God. But did you read

about how those women suffered? I admire and respect the women who are doing their best to make their marriages work because they honor the vows that they made before God. Some women did not have the benefit of godly counsel; they were not saved or did not know the biblical principles of marriage. Other women were counseled against marrying certain men, but they did it anyway and some of them have regretted their decision to ignore wise counsel. I do not recommend that any woman set out to change a man. I don't see that example modeled in scripture. Abigail was married to a foolish man and she had to clean up his mistakes (1 Sam. 25). How exhausting and annoying that must have been! I don't believe that we need to experience everything in order to become wise. I believe we can learn from the mistakes of others. A wise woman told me, "There are some testimonies that you just don't need to have."

There are too many testimonies about the sadness that results from being unequally yoked or being with a person who does not compliment your purpose. Nowhere in the bible is it recommended that a woman take on a man as her DIY project. Nowhere in the bible are you told to fix the man. It is the Holy Spirit's job to bring conviction. Yes, the saved wife sanctifies the unsaved husband (1 Cor. 7:14), but have you talked to Christian women who are enduring in marriages with unsaved men? Do you know the sorrow in their hearts? Do you know the disappointment when they get a revelation from God, but they can't share it with their husbands because they are uninterested? Do you know the burden that a woman carries when her husband is not the priest, prophet and king of the home? Do you know the pain of living with a prayerless husband? A husband who won't or can't cover his wife and family with intercessory prayers? Do you know how lonely and forsaken a woman feels when she goes to church and her husband stays at home? Do you know the heartache these women endure?

Yes, God can use you as instrument to change him, but how worn down will your health become? How much premature aging will be added to your face and body? How much life will be drained from you? How much damage will be done to your esteem while you compensate for his underdevelopment, cruelty, lack of concern or understanding? How many stress lines will be added to your face? Have you read about the women of God who prayed and prayed, but their husbands refused to change? ? Have you heard about the men who changed after their wives died or became deathly ill? Why would you set yourself up for such a traumatic lifestyle when you can avoid such drama?

    Nowhere in the bible is it recommended that a woman seek a man that she has to change. A man has to be husband material already. In a godly marriage, the husband and wife will grow together and learn from each other, but the man should have some qualifying traits as a single person. He has to be fit for marriage before you say, "I do". Is the man that you admire prepared to wash you with the water of the Word? (Eph. 5:26) Is he capable and willing to sacrifice his time for you? Is he able to pray for you, intercede on your behalf, or call down fire from Heaven if need be?

    Adam, Moses, Abraham, Isaac and Jacob had a personal relationship with God before they were married. Jesus is the best example of a bridegroom since he sacrificed his life for the church. Born-again believers are the bride of Christ. Jesus loves us and he demonstrates his love through his sacrifice and intercessory prayer along with his role as mediator, healer and deliverer. Remember, how you start a relationship is usually how you must continue it. If you start out being the teacher and the revelator, you will probably have to continue in that role until Jesus returns. The bible says that the man is the head of the wife (1 Cor. 11:3). How can he lead you if he does not have leadership ability? How can you follow someone who is blind or not interested in receiving his sight? You can try to change him, but you won't be following God's original design for courtship and marriage. You will be usurping the Holy Spirit's role. Begin the way you want to end. Let God bring a man who will lead you in the paths of righteousness. Lean not unto thine own understanding, but in all your ways acknowledge Him and He will direct your paths (Prov. 3:5-6). If you choose to be God, then you are responsible for the outcome. Let God be in charge, apply his principles and leave the rest up to Him.

It Could Be Worse
It could be worse, but it can also be better. Suppose you hear about a man who beats his girlfriend, curses at his children and physically abuses them, refuses to pay any bills, spends all of his money on video games, the race track, clothes and liquor. He dates other women and parades them in front of his girlfriend. One person counsels the woman to leave him immediately while another "friend" advises her to "Hang in there because it could be worse." And may I add, it can and usually does get worse.

"It could be worse" is a poor excuse to remain in a toxic relationship. When a woman remains in an abusive relationship she usually feels helpless, trapped, inferior, and worthless. Sometimes she remains in the relationship because she thinks if she just hangs in there a little longer, he will change and he might, but what will she have lost in the process. Sometimes, hanging in there could cost her to lose her life. If she doesn't lose her life, she becomes a shell of a person unrecognizable to family and friends. Sometimes she remains with an abusive man because she received poor advice. She may believe that this is the best she can do so she settles for a destructive relationship. She settles for what is familiar because of the thought, "What if I never find anybody else?" She rarely thinks of other possibilities like "What if there's someone who will treat me better?" "What if I let go of him and pursue my goals?" She could get that college degree or start that business that she always dreamed of. She could renew her relationship with the Lord or get to know Him as Lord and Savior.

What if the man you're dating is blocking you from meeting the person you can actually be happy with? Worse yet, what if the man you're dating with is preventing you from fulfilling the purpose that God ordained for your life? And what if the man you're dating never changes or you never grow or develop into the person that God intended you to be? Wouldn't it be sad to get to Heaven and discover that God had so much more for you, but you limited yourself with the excuse, "It could be worse." Yes, it could be worse, but it can also be better. Seek to make your life better. Discover your life's purpose and begin to pursue that.

Maybe you're accustomed to being hurt in relationships. You believe that all of the good men are taken so you've settled for leftovers. You've accepted chaos as the norm. You've tried to find ways to cope with the dysfunction. Maybe you have even created your own person in your mind to numb yourself to the reality of your relationship. So you're dating Mark, but you're pretending that he has Ron's boyish charm, Michael's sense of humor and William's good looks. You're used to being drained after conversations because he has sucked the life out of you with his co-dependent ways. You've accepted his self-centered ways where all conversations begin and end with him as the focal point. Dysfunction has become normal. Crazy has become comfortable, but you are not alone and you can be free from the confusion.

Whether you're reading this book because you're questioning your relationship, searching for help for yourself or someone else or just wanting to learn more about soul ties, you took a courageous step and you're ready for the truth. It takes two people to be in a toxic relationship. If you've read this far, you are ready to get rid of the "crazy in you" and disconnect from the "crazy in him".

2
Signs of a Toxic Relationship/Soul Tie

COMPROMISE - I THINK this is one of the biggest indicators of a soul tie. You can tell that you are compromising when you lower your standards. For instance, you used to believe that dating a married man was wrong, but when you found out he was married, you continued the affair anyway. You used to believe that a man should have a job, business or at least be looking for one, but now you pay his bills and he drives your car. You used to believe that sex before marriage was wrong, but since you've been dating this guy, you've changed your mind. You never watched X-rated movies until you started dating him. He introduced you to pornography and you violated your own conscience to please him. Or maybe you've compromised your devotional time. You had an established, intimate prayer and worship life, but now you rarely pray or read the bible.

Dishonors God – When you're in a soul tie, the man you're dating becomes your god. You care more about his opinion than what God thinks about a matter. In essence, you are worshipping the created more than the Creator (Rom. 1:25). You are dishonoring God. The bible says that thou shalt have no other God before Him because He is a jealous God. (Ex. 20:3, Deut. 5:7) You can honor and respect your man, but only God is to be worshipped.

Lack of Peace – You have a troubled conscience. God has given us a conscience to help us distinguish between right and wrong (Rom. 2:15). When we ignore our conscience, we are ignoring one of the God-created safety mechanisms. Also, if you have the Holy Spirit, you can feel when you have grieved the Holy Spirit, which will make you very sad. (Eph. 4:30).

Insomnia - You lay down to sleep, but your conscience doesn't allow you to sleep. You have difficulty falling or remaining asleep. There is a nagging at your conscience that inhibits your ability to rest. The bible says that God has written truth on our hearts, in our conscience (Rom. 2:15). Your entire sleep pattern is changed or interrupted. You're restless and your sleep is erratic. There is a general lack of peace. Your conscience nags at your soul. You may also suffer from frequent stomach upsets. Your sleep is erratic or interrupted by your own guilty conscience. You may sleep, but you don't get rest because your soul is disturbed. The Lord says, "Come unto me all ye that labour and are heavy-laden and I will give you rest" (Matt. 11:28).

Mental Confusion – Your thoughts are cloudy. You can only think or complete one task at a time, which is strange considering that multi-tasking is a common trait among most women. I refer to this condition as "brain fog." You're confused because the relationship is confusing. You're unsure of his love because his actions or lack of action raise concerns. For instance, when he needs help you're always available, but he doesn't extend the same courtesy to you. He offers an explanation for his "missing-in-action," but you don't understand his lack of commitment.

Stress – Worry and anxiety have become your best friend. You over think everything. "If I wear this outfit, will he like it?" You censor your words before you speak. "If I say…, will he become offended?" "If I respond in this tone of voice, will he give me the silent treatment or make sarcastic comments?" Basically, you're walking on eggshells. You've become a basket case trying to make sure that you don't offend him. You're full of fear, worry, anxiety and doubt. You are stressed out.

Nervous Stomach – Your stomach twists and turns. Sometimes, you have to go to the bathroom as soon as you hear HIS voice or get in his presence. Just the thought of the him can trigger a nervous stomach.

A Drain On Your Emotions – When you're around him or soon after you leave his presence or hang up the phone, you feel drained, tired and lethargic. He's siphoning gas from your fuel tank. He is the hose and your energy is the fuel. In all fairness to him, he may be unaware of his life-sucking tendencies. Nevertheless, your encounters with him leave you dry.

Denial and Desperation– Everything is okay at first, but then you begin to notice that he has a lot of female "friends". He is never where he says he will be. He is unavailable at certain hours of the night although he has a day job and he isn't at a prayer meeting. When he speaks to his "friends," he excuses himself from your presence so he can take the call in private. Without warning, he explains that he had to cut dinner short because of an emergency. The truth is that this guy is a player, but you so desperately want to believe his lies that you continue in the relationship anyway.

Disrespect - You are disrespected. He says he will call or show up at a certain time, but he doesn't keep his word. He makes excuses to justify his behavior or he doesn't apologize at all and continues to demonstrate a blatant disregard for your feelings. He may even insult the way you dress or make fun of your personality or value system.

Lowered Self-Esteem - When you're around him, your esteem drops to the basement. You feel inferior or confused. You never feel fully accepted by him. Your flaws are emphasized or blown out of proportion. He may even try to redo your wardrobe, make-up, jewelry or other accessories. He may like isolated things about you. For instance, he may enjoy your smile, but hate the way you laugh. Maybe he likes your personality, but dislikes your body structure.

Lack of Joy – Soul ties steals your joy. You're sad and moping all of the time, but you don't know why. You were a bubbly, outgoing woman, but with the passing of time in this relationship you became sullen and withdrawn.

You become his therapist. You become his problem solver and therapist. His problems become your problems and his problems are monumental, intense and tall as a skyscraper. That's a lot of weight on you now, but you have nowhere to drop it off because he is ill-equipped to handle his own problems so he dumps them on you. The challenge is that when you have a problem, he can't help you because his problems never end. His lists of problems get longer, bigger and stronger. While your problems mount up, but they are never addressed. Stress lines, wrinkles, and a sad face become your usual look. You may look like you've aged 10 years since being in the relationship.

Your dignity is violated. He embarrasses you about things you can't control, things like your bone structure, height, skin color or facial features. He may even insult or look with disdain at your choice of clothes, jewelry, make-up or hairstyle. He will even label you as an idiot or stupid to describe the decisions that you make.

Your reasoning ability is blocked and your will is stifled. You know you shouldn't go to his house, but you go anyway. An invisible magnet keeps pulling you toward him. You know you shouldn't spend so much time on the phone, but you do it anyway and important things like paying bills, grocery shopping and household chores don't get done. Your thinking is muddled and cloudy. All you can seem to think about is him and nothing else. It's like your brain is in a fog.

Embarrassment - When you're around him, you feel humiliated, awkward or inferior. He makes you feel ashamed of yourself. He is never satisfied with your appearance, your style of dress, the way you speak or the way you wear your hair. He compares you to other women or tries to transform you into his vision of an ideal woman. He may even attempt to mold you into the person that he desires with no regard or appreciation for your individuality. In essence, you become his project or Barbie doll. He will redefine you, which will limit you. You can only be yourself and you will always fail at being someone else. In essence, you are never good enough in his eyesight. And if you're not careful, you'll end up rejecting yourself based on his opinion. *You are God's creation! Who is he to reject what God made?* I know I'm supposed to be sharing the signs of a soul tie, but I had to remind you of who you are. Okay, let's get back to the list.

Weight Gain – You don't only gain physical weight, but you also accumulate emotional baggage. You end up carrying the luggage of his past relationships, hurts and disappointments. It feels like he has dumped a pile of blankets on you and is forcing you to carry them around with you all day and all night. He weighs down your spirit, makes your soul fat with depression and changes your attitude for the worst. You may even experience weight gain as you try to eat away his problems and yours.

A Sense Of Loss - You may lose several things including your ability to focus, your strength, energy, determination, motivation, appetite, weight, sleep and hair.

Loss of Focus - One of the first things that a soul tie will rob you of is focus. You find it difficult to concentrate on any task for a sustained period of time. It's difficult to complete daily activities. It's like your brain is in a fog and mental fatigue sets in. Simple things like reading a book or performing a task at work become interrupted with thoughts of "What is my 'boo' doing? How is he feeling?" I know what you're thinking, "Isn't that normal?" Not when your thoughts are continually interrupted. Not when you can't get anything done on time or in an organized way. You spend an excessive amount of time with him to the point where hardly nothing else gets done. He takes priority and everything else takes a backseat including your personal care. The sink is piled up with dishes, the garbage can needs to be dumped, the laundry basket is overflowing, the bathroom is long overdue for a cleaning – all because you can't focus. Your mind is occupied with your "boo" constantly.

Loss of Energy - Have you noticed a loss in your strength? When you finally do start your "to-do" list, you don't have the energy to complete your tasks. It seems like something zapped all of your energy. You've noticed that you're extremely tired lately and you weren't tired before you started dating him. You are physically weak especially after you talk to him in person or on the phone. You find that after the conversation is over, it feels like a vacuum sucked all of the energy out of you and you need to take a nap in order to recover your strength. You think you need to increase your intake of B-12 vitamins, but it's more than that. He is a drain on your physical energy because he absorbs most of your time and his conversation may be boring or self-centered most of the time.

You have become his therapist. Therefore, most of your conversation is focused on him. He talks about his problems or victories and vents about his low points in life. You pour all of your mother wit and sage advice into him until when the conversation is over you are physically drained. Oh and if you're a prayer warrior, men like this will really drain you. Men like this need lots of prayer. You will pray down fire from heaven for their deliverance, healing and breakthrough, but when it's your turn they are often unable or unwilling to reciprocate. So you have to fill his cup and your own cup. How exhausting and unbalanced is that?!!!

Decreased Motivation - You were motivated and had set goals for yourself, but now your only goal is to please him. You put all of your goals on hold. You had plans to start a business, continue your college education, join a gym, eat healthier foods, improve your devotion time with the Lord, take a sewing class or write a book. You abandoned all of your goals for one aim – to please him. All of your time was transferred to helping him achieve his goals. There are several problems with this approach. He is not your husband. He has not proven that he is worthy to become your husband. A godly man wants you to be the best you can be and wants to assist in helping you fulfill your goals. He would never want you to abandon your dreams to support his.

Loss of Appetite - You lose your appetite. The first time I lost my appetite during a soul tie I really didn't pay any attention until a friend through God's revelation told me that my weight loss was due to my association with a particular individual. I was involved in an ungodly soul tie, but I didn't know it; I had overextended myself in my dealings with this person and I had failed to draw boundaries. As a result, most of my time was occupied helping this individual which left me with little to no energy to take care of myself. Years later, I met someone and began to experience weight loss again as a result of my association with this man. I thought that he might be a potential mate. This time the weight loss was very obvious to me. There was a drastic difference with this soul tie. I lost my appetite and dropped a significant amount of weight within two weeks. I also noticed that I was losing focus. I couldn't think about anything except this man. I am a foodie and any time I lose the desire for food something is definitely wrong. I could go 5-7 hours without eating and not even miss food. That's when I started reflecting on what was going on with me. What I didn't understand at the time was that this was my body's way of responding to this toxic relationship.

Transference – The other weird thing that started happening is that I started having an increase in lustful thoughts and I started wondering, "Where are these thoughts coming from?" Have you ever heard of the scripture, "Bad company corrupts good character" (1 Cor. 15:33). Well, hanging around the wrong people can produce bad fruit in your life. When the relationship between this man and I ended, I no longer had those lustful thoughts. Thank you Jesus! In other words, his demons started to affect me.

When I was a child, people would always caution my generation to be careful who we chose as friends. At the time, I didn't see what the big deal was, but when I started experiencing thoughts that I had been delivered from, I realized that being around this man did not lead me to further godliness, but it heightened lust in my mind.

Spiritual Blindness - You can't see that you're spiraling downward. You're in a fog. You're not even aware that you're being manipulated. You definitely can't see how the enemy is using your vulnerability to his advantage. Your weakness has become a playing field for the enemy and a stronghold in your life. A stronghold is a strong structure for keeping something in or out. In this case, the devil's lies form a fortress around your mind. This stronghold keeps the truth out and locks the lie into your mind and heart. Your soul is in prison, but you are spiritually blind about the soul-damaging relationship. You don't recognize that he is causing you to go backwards in life or become stagnate. You don't even realize that you have been sidetracked. You've placed all of your goals aside and decided to play "wifey" to someone who hasn't even committed to being your spouse. He just utters smooth words in that direction, but he hasn't made any concrete commitments, but you're all in. He may have even shown obvious signs of his dislike for you or an inability to love you unconditionally, but you think he'll grow to love you as time passes.

Loss Of Your Will – You have an inability to say, "No." You call him excessively and you know you shouldn't be on the phone for hours at a time, but you do it anyway. You drop everything you're doing when he calls. He gets everything done, but you miss deadlines and appointments. It's as if you have no power to resist, no power to say, "No." You go to his house more than you should. You lack self-control. There is no balance. He literally becomes the center of your world.

Sexual Sin- Sexual sin will make the soul tie even stronger. You were already involved in an unhealthy emotional, mental or spiritual connection. Now you have become physically connected to the person which makes it more difficult to think clearly and to separate from the manipulation. Illegal sexual activity is a door to trouble. Sex outside of marriage is spiritually illegal. As believers we are to present our bodies as living sacrifices (Rom. 12:1). Promiscuity can be treacherous and life-altering for the believer as well as the unbeliever. How many times have you heard of stories where people were promiscuous and they had nothing to show for it, but a ruined life, twisted emotions, and sexually transmitted diseases? Your body is important and God does not want you to abuse it. Samson thought that he was just having a sexual encounter, but what he didn't know was that the enemy was setting him up for a fall.

3
What is a Soul Tie?

FIRST, I NEED to correct a false statement that I've read and heard quite frequently. The myth is that a soul tie must involve sex. While sex cements a soul tie, it is not a necessary ingredient. Cults create soul ties by manipulating a person's soul (mind, emotions and will). Some cults operate without ever introducing an element of sex. In short, cults use mind control to dominate their members. The person's soul is controlled by the cult leader and the doctrine of their organization. The same thing happens in a relationship with a human being. Without ever participating in sex, your soul can be controlled. However, if sex is introduced into the relationship, the bond becomes stronger. The next pages will illustrate the definition and signs of a soul tie.

A soul tie is a relationship that can be positive or negative. Positive soul ties enhance you, your relationships and your endeavors. They make you a better person. They improve your friendships, marriage, business, ministry and/or work. They energize and motivate you. For instance, a relationship in which both a man and woman respect and encourage each other is positive. They benefit from each other in a healthy and godly manner. On the other hand, a negative soul tie damages your well-being and strains all of your other relationships. They drain you. One or both people in the relationship lose their identity, become a doormat or compromise their values. This kind of soul tie poisons, twists and manipulates the soul and drains the life, joy and peace from one or both people in the relationship. Simply put, this kind of soul tie occurs when your soul is dominated by another person. In this book, the phrase soul tie refers to a toxic or unhealthy relationship.

Let's examine the word "soul". Your soul is invisible and it is made up of three parts – your mind, will and emotions. In an ungodly soul tie, your thoughts, decisions and feelings are held hostage. Your mind consists of your thoughts. Your thoughts can be positive or negative. Your will is the part of you that has the ability to choose. For example, sometimes you don't feel like going to work but by an act of your will, you tell yourself that you will go to work and you get up out of your bed. You will it to be so. In that case, you use your willpower. Your emotions, on the other hand, are your feelings. Feelings can be fickle. One day we feel great and the next day we don't feel great. One day we feel like eating popcorn and the next day we don't feel like eating popcorn. A soul tie occurs when your thoughts, will and emotions are manipulated by another person.

Now, let's define the word "tie". A tie is a knot, connection, or bond. Therefore, a soul tie occurs when your soul (your mind, will, and emotions) is super-glued to the soul of another person. In other words, your mind, will, and emotions are bonded to the thoughts, will and emotions of another person in the form of a friendship, romantic, business and/or ministry partnership. In this book, the phrase soul tie will refer to negative relationships.

Remember that invisible magnet that I mentioned in the introduction of this book. A soul tie can also be compared to a magnet. Have you ever purchased a magnetic decoration for your refrigerator? If you hold the magnet in your hand and slowly move it toward the refrigerator door, you feel the pull of the magnet toward the door's surface. In this scenario, the magnet represents you while the door symbolizes your "boo". You are drawn deeper into the relationship although you may really want to pull away. If you can learn to identify the signs of toxic relationships or the red flags of potential mates, you can prevent a lot of heartache. Let's look at three examples of a soul tie.

Examples of Soul Ties

Tony showed Angela lots of attention. He called her several times throughout the day and spent long hours at night on the telephone. Angela always dropped whatever she was doing to meet Tony's every need and to answer all of his telephone calls. He occupied so much of Angela's time that Angela slipped up on her responsibilities. She barely got her laundry done, dishes washed, garbage dumped, or bills paid on time. Her job performance was negatively impacted by this relationship. She was tired and unable to focus because of all the time and attention she devoted to Tony. She barely talked to any of her friends or family anymore because she was consumed with Tony. When she did talk to family and friends every conversation was about Tony.

Angela also gave up on all of her goals and began to focus on helping Tony achieve his career and ministry goals. As a result, Angela became extremely depressed, but she didn't know why. She thought that she had done all that a good girlfriend should do. Why wasn't she happy?

She wasn't happy because she was unfulfilled, had forsaken her goals and lost her identity. Tony had dominated her soul. A man should never take the place of God. He should enhance your relationship with the Father. Your association with him should not derail you from your goals or strip you of your identity. Angela thought she was being a dutiful girlfriend, but the truth is that she was participating in the ruin of her own soul.

Consider the soul tie of Lisa and James. Lisa was a worship leader at her church and James headed the youth ministry at his church. The two met through a mutual friend. They had an instant connection because of their work in ministry. Lisa shared information about her past relationships, the mistakes she made and the shortcomings of the guys she dated. James was impressed with her honesty and assumed that she must be the one. Lisa had also shared that she had difficulty remaining faithful and was looking for "the one" to whom she could commit.

As Lisa shared more secrets with James, she praised him for being a good listener, explaining that she could marry someone like him. James thought he was "the one". After several months, Lisa ended the relationship abruptly with an explanation that left James wondering where he had gone wrong.

Lisa had deep trust issues and would never be able to commit to anyone until her insecurities were addressed. Lisa had dominated James' soul. James let his guard down and ignored the truth. Lisa told him that she had trouble being faithful. That was a red flag, but James ignored it.

Tonya and Michael were the perfect couple. They both loved and enjoyed the word of God. They both loved and enjoyed worship music. They had the same career interests – business and marketing. They were both heavily involved in ministry within their church. They spent long hours on the phone in the word of God, long hours singing worship songs and praying.

Tonya occupied a lot of Michael's time during the week and on weekends. Michael would try to hang up so that he could run errands and do things that he enjoyed, but Tonya would beg him not to hang up and sometimes insist that he stay on the phone with her because she was not ready to end the conversation.

Pretty soon, Michael became sluggish. He didn't understand why his energy seemed to be depleted every time he spoke to Tonya on the phone or in person. He just thought he needed to take more vitamins or eat more vegetables. He didn't realize that Tonya was draining the life out of him with her co-dependent ways.

Tonya had abandonment issues. She had been exposed to numerous tragedies. Her best friend died in middle school, her boyfriend died in a car accident in high school and her father died while she was away at college and she was afraid that Michael would leave her like all of the other people she loved. As a result, she suffocated Michael with her clingy ways. Fear was the motivating force behind Tonya's actions. Tonya had dominated Michael's soul.

Think about your current and past relationships. Do any of these relationships remind you of similar experiences? What was the glue that connected these soul ties? Time and imagination. Notice how in each instance the couples spent a lot of time together. A soul tie requires a doorway. Time is that gateway. The person has to have a way to get into your mind, emotions, or will. The quickest way to subdue a person's soul is through conversation and physical presence. They need the opportunity to talk to you on the phone, through text, social media or in person. The longer a person occupies your time, the deeper they get into your thoughts, feelings and decisions.

The second factor is imagination. If a man can get you to believe that you are "the chosen one" or if you've convinced yourself that you are "the one", you will drop your guard and let the man into your heart. As the man showers you with compliments like, "I always wanted to meet someone like you." "You are such a good listener." "I can be myself when I'm with you." "I wish I had met you a long time ago." "I could see myself married to you." These are wonderful comments, but these are deadly comments from someone who is broken, deceptive, unstable or immature.

Soul ties are so dangerous because even when the relationship is over, your souls are still tied together. Even though you and the other person have moved on, it's as if you're still together unless you break the ties (See chapter 17). That's why we really need to choose wisely because the wrong choice leaves trash in our souls.

Here's another analogy that might help you better understand a soul tie. Imagine a rope tied around your hands and feet. Now visualize your suitor holding the end of the rope in his hand and pulling it in any direction he chooses. What happens to you as he pulls the rope? You guessed it. You are controlled by him and you must follow wherever he leads you. Replace the physical ropes with invisible ropes.

These are the invisible cords that connect you to his moods, whims and desires. The influence may be subtle or obvious.

In other words, the effect of the toxic relationship sneaks up on you or slaps you in the face. It may take several days, weeks or months for the effects of the soul tie to manifest. Whatever the timeframe, the results are the same. Your thoughts, feelings and will are not your own. They are being controlled by the mood and desire of someone else.

Friends and family look at your relationship and wonder why you don't detach yourself. They can't see the invisible ropes and neither can you, but they can see the negative impact that the relationship is having on you. You look like a zombie. Your loved ones see the loss of joy and individuality, the emptiness in your eyes, the fake smiles, the lowered self-esteem, the weight loss or weight gain, the loss of focus and increased irritability and frustration.

You and I know that we are not wrestling against flesh and blood, but against principalities, rulers of darkness and spiritual wickedness in high places (Eph. 6:12). It is not the person doing the evil, but the spirit operating in the person. God does not want you to be ignorant of the devil's devices (2 Cor. 2:11). You must guard your heart against the evil that is coming through the person.

Soul ties are not always obvious because they consist of invisible components. You can't see a person's thoughts, emotions or will. You can only see the expression of their soul through their words and actions. Their conversation and behavior reveal the kind of thoughts, emotions and will power that they possess. There are many ways that a man gains control over your soul. He can use sex, conversation and other strategies to manipulate you. Most of the time, the methods are subtle, but strategic. As believers we know that the real enemy behind all of this wickedness is the devil. I like to expose his tactics.

When a person controls another person, the outcome is always negative because God never intended human beings to dominate each other. He told Adam and Eve to have dominion over the earth and the fish of the sea and the fowl of the air (Gen. 1:28). Some men will try to convince you that leadership and domination are the same. Leadership is when a man leads by example. For instance, he shows you what respect is like by being respectful. He shows you what kindness is like by being kind. Domination is the opposite. A dominating man demands respect, but rarely gives it. He is often rude and controlling. He speaks in demanding tones such as, "You will respect me and do what I say!" That man is operating under a controlling spirit. He wants to dominate you. That is ungodly. God never told Adam to rule over Eve.

Submission is not permission for domination. Man was designed to dominate his environment. Even God Himself, as powerful and mighty as He is, does not force us to love Him. He demonstrates His love and it is His love that draws us (Jer. 31:3). A man should draw you to him through his sincere love and sacrifice for you. Some fathers and husbands have confused leadership with domination. As a result, their wives and daughters have been confused about what male leadership looks and feels like. That's why it is so easy for some women to be duped into thinking that a controlling man is a strong man when in reality a controlling man is an insecure man.

The devil, the enemy of our souls wants to get us off track and cause us to lust after someone and be involved in sexual relationships outside of marriage. The devil wants to get a foothold into your life. Sex outside of marriage is one of the ways that he gains entrance into your life. He wants to get one foot into your life and his entire nature into your soul. That's why the Bible says, "Give no place to the devil." (Eph. 4:7) Don't give him any space in your life. His aim is to destroy you.

Soul ties form such a strong attachment that you find yourself doing things you never thought you would do. You find yourself going places that you never thought you would go. You find yourself saying things that you never thought you would say and that's because you are involved in a soul tie.

This kind of bonding distorts your perception and clouds your thoughts, leaving your mind in a fog of confusion and doubt. That's the thing about soul ties. They blind you spiritually so that you don't know what to think anymore.

Let me give you another example. You've heard of women who are battered or physically, emotionally, mentally or spiritually abused and/or manipulated. As observers we ask ourselves, "Can't she see that he's crazy?" "Can't she see that he's abusive?" "Why doesn't she just get up and leave him?" Her soul is roped to his soul.

A wicked attachment is perverting her perception. What she thought was wrong prior to the relationship is what she is now embracing. She tolerates disrespect now as if it's normal. Her mind, will and emotions are intimately connected, attached, or cemented to his soul. Her thoughts revolve around him all day long. She thinks about how she can please him and how she can keep him from getting angry. She thinks about how she can keep him satisfied. Her will has been completely surrendered to his will. This is a perversion of submission. Submission should never render you powerless, unable to focus or cause you to worship a man.

You can form an emotional soul tie with a married man. You and he can talk on the phone, at work or as a neighbor. You share personal stories and opinions in person, through text, face time or social media. This is a type of soul tie. Beware. This is dangerous. Most affairs start this way. Soul ties start with conversation and spending time with a person. Besides, you are not his wife. He should be cleaving to his wife (Gen. 2:24; Matt. 19:5), sharing his personal experiences, opinions and emotions with the person he made a life-long commitment to.

4
Comfortable with Crazy

IF YOU LINE up all of your ex-boyfriends in a row, you can see the flow chart of your mental illness. A funny and truthful statement! What made me date him? What was I thinking? The problem is that neither you nor I were thinking clearly when we chose certain people. Either we didn't have God's wisdom or we ignored His wisdom in favor of our own fleshly desires. Our thinking was twisted. This leads me to my next topic of discussion. At times we are quick to judge other women for their choice in men, unable to understand their bondage, but we shouldn't be so quick to point out their flawed decision-making when we've made some choices that even make us scratch our heads. You know how you look at old pictures of someone you used to date and you think to yourself, "What was I thinking?" Read on to discover why some women don't leave a man who is so obviously unfit and underserving of their attention and affection.

Why Doesn't She Leave?
Why does a woman stay in a relationship with a man who is abusive? It's typically because her will has been completely surrendered to his will. She no longer has the ability to choose. The rational part of her brain doesn't function. Her reasoning ability is blocked along with her emotions. Now she is depressed. Her esteem is so low that she

doesn't think like a sensible person. Therefore, she is in a soul tie and it takes the power and love of God to really bring her out of that.

She will often experience symptoms like knots in her stomach, moments of repeated confusion, inability to make a decision and stick to it, the feeling of being in a fog and utter loss of control. Like the woman in the scenario below, you and I knew something was wrong, but we didn't have a name for it. You know that your relationships are unhealthy and always follow the same patterns and cycles of defeat, but you didn't know why.

The Wrestling Match
To further illustrate the bondage of a soul tie, let me create a mental picture of what's going on with your soul when it's bound by invisible ropes. Visualize two people wrestling. Eventually one wrestler gets the upper hand and successfully subdues his opponent, pinning him to the canvas. The weaker opponent struggles, squirms and fights to defeat his opponent, but is unable to get up. The more skilled opponent gets the best of the feeble opponent. In this scenario, the stronger wrestler represents the man who pins unsuspecting women to the floor, thus making her soul his playpen. This is what the enemy wants to do to people. This is why we must guard our heart (Prov. 4:23). We should never haphazardly or carelessly give it away.

The bottom line is that the enemy desires that we never fulfill our purpose, but there is a greater power than our adversary and His name is Jesus Christ. He tells us that we cannot enter a strong man's house until we first tie him up. (Matt. 12:29, Mark 3:27) What is keeping you in this relationship? Let's tie up that spirit so you can go free? What is holding you there? Lust? Fear? Desperation? Loneliness? Confusion?

Although there is not a physical cord that ties you to this man, there is a supernatural connection of your soul to his soul. These invisible ropes cause you to lose control of your decision-making ability and now all of your decisions are based on this man. You may say that love is sacrificial and there's nothing wrong with putting his well-being before yours. The problem is that he has become the center of your world at your expense. Only God is to be worshipped. The man you idolize gets all the benefits while you lose your self-worth. It's time to regain your respect and your dignity.

Jesus came to set the captives free. In Acts 16:26, the very foundations of the prison were shaken and the captives were set free after Paul and Silas prayed and sang unto the Lord. God wants to break the shackles and destroy the foundation that has kept you trapped in an emotional, mental and spiritual prison. It's time to break out. You can be free. You were not created to be enslaved - trapped in your emotions. You were created to live the abundant life freely in Christ Jesus. After you have given your life to the Lord, you are entitled to heavenly benefits. It's like being a member of an exclusive club. Once you join, you are entitled to certain privileges and benefits that non-members don't get. It is a privilege to be a believer. As a member of the heavenly kingdom, you have the right to be free. Soul ties chain your emotions, your mind and your will. Be set free by the power of the Lord Jesus Christ today!

The Making of a Soul Tie
Let's examine the soul tie of a man and woman in the bible. The man's name is Samson and the woman's name is Delilah. Let me introduce you to a man named Samson. The first thing I want to point out is that Samson's birth was not accidental. His life was ordained. God chose him for a special assignment before his mother conceived him.

We are often careless about our choices because we don't understand that we were born on purpose for a purpose. God has a plan for your life. He created this plan before you were formed in your mother's womb (Jer. 1:5). Your life is bigger than you. It has a greater meaning. You were not born to please yourself. Like Samson, you were born to please God and carry out His mission for your life. You will find great joy and peace in carrying out the will of the Lord for your life.

Before Samson was conceived, God sent an angel to tell his mother that she would give birth to a child who would have a special assignment from the Lord. The angel said that Samson would be born as a Nazarite. Nazarites had to follow certain requirements as a demonstration of their commitment to God. Samson could not cut his hair, drink wine or come in contact with dead bodies. God orchestrated a covenant between he and Samson by requiring him to never cut his hair. As long as he honored the agreement, he would always have power over his enemies.

The Nazarite covenant is not much different from the covenant that God makes with believers. There are things that God asks us not to do as a demonstration to the world that we belong to Him and are committed to living a holy life. For example, He asks all Christians to save sex for marriage. He does not ask this to rob us of joy. Our heavenly Father asks this to protect us from soul-damage. God orchestrated Samson's birth and designed his life's purpose before his mother was intimate with his father. This proves that God knew us before we were formed in our mother's womb and has plans for our lives (Jer. 29:11).

The enemy wanted to destroy Samson because he was anointed from birth. That means he had a special call on his life. Samson was a very strong man. His strength was a gift from God. He had supernatural strength like Superman. He uprooted the city gates of Gaza and carried it on his shoulders to the top of the hill facing Hebron (Judges 16:3). Gaza was one of 5 Philistine royal cities that was heavily fortified. The city gate was probably about 60 feet high and archaeological evidence indicates that city gates in this period in time were usually made from parallel pairs of massive stone blocks. The posts and bar would probably have been solid cedar. Overall, we're talking tons of weight! Samson carried the gate to Hebron. The nearest hill facing Hebron is 37 miles away! Not only that, Hebron (later, an Israelite royal city) was Israel's highest city above sea level, so the hill would have been one of the highest points in Israel. So the gate of their enemy's royal city was sitting on top of a hill for all the Israelites from miles around to see! What an insult and embarrassment to the Philistines! This amazing feat by Samson demonstrates God's greatness and power over His people's enemies. He had the ability to whip groups or thousands of men with his bare hands (Judges 14:19; 15:15). He could fight animals and win with his bare hands (Judges 14:6). This was the anointing of God, strength that was put upon Samson because he was empowered by God.

5
Seducing Spirits

Snake Eyes
HAVE YOU EVER seen the cartoons where the snake rises out of a basket and hypnotizes its prey with its eyes? A soul tie puts you in a trance just like a snake charmer controls a serpent. The bible describes people who are deceived by others as being under the control of a seducing spirit (1Timothy 4:1). When you're in a soul tie, you're in a trance. You are being controlled and manipulated by an evil spirit operating through a person.

When Samson had sex with Delilah, he became hypnotized in the same manner that Eve was seduced by the serpent (Gen. 3: 4-6). Seduction means to be deceived or tricked by a person, Satan, sin or darkness. It means to beguile or deceive; to be deceived into an illusion. It happens when a person is tricked into believing a lie. You are lured to biting the bait, but you don't know that there's a hook beneath the bait that will ruin your jaw. That's the outcome of deception. You miss the truth because you focused on an illusion.

Influence Equals Eye-fluence
Seduction often involves flattery and an appeal to one or more of the senses. Satan seduced Eve by appealing to the lust of her eyes. Eve was influenced by what she saw. The strategies of the enemy never

change. He seeks control through the lust of the flesh, the lust of the eyes or the pride of life (1 John 2:16). We can ask God to anoint our eyes with eye salve so that we see as God sees. We can also live a godly life which serves as protection against being controlled or influenced by Satan. We are not to lust after people. We can admire their beauty, but we should never lust after people. Lust is an excessive desire. It is a craving that is out of control and usually results in disorderly or immoral behavior.

Satan enticed Eve by causing her to focus on the physical appearance of the fruit of the tree of knowledge and good and evil. (Gen. 3:6). It's one thing to have a passing thought, but danger creeps in when we become consumed or taken over by an ungodly thought. The enemy caused her to meditate on it. He further deceived her with the power of persuasion. He told her that she would be wise like the most high God (Gen. 3:5), but she was already occupying a place of preeminence. She was in daily communion and fellowship with God's first son and she was partaker of the inside scoop, the inside job that God was doing. She had access to the choicest real estate – the Garden of Eden.

Sometimes the enemy will make you think that you're missing something when in reality you aren't missing anything. What you have is greater than what the enemy is trying to offer. What the enemy offers is short-lived, but what you have with Christ is permanent. Never trade your relationship with Christ for empty promises. Eve became hypnotized by the good-looking fruit. She was deceived by the lie that the fruit would make her wise. She was already wise. She was living with the God of the universe and he had given her everything. What more could she ask for? And so it is with us. We have everything in Christ. Have we taken the time to appreciate God for what he has already given us?

Under A Spell
Delilah seduced Samson with her body. Sex with her became his drug. He was addicted to their sexual encounters which allowed Delilah to

completely deceive him. He was under her spell and captivated by the forbidden fruit. "Now the Spirit speaketh expressly, that in the latter times some shall depart from the faith, giving heed to seducing spirits, and doctrines of devils." (1 Timothy 4:1) "The righteous should choose his friends carefully for the way of the wicked will seduce them (lead them astray). (Proverbs 12:26). But evil men and seducers (impostors) shall wax worse and worse, deceiving and being deceived. (2 Tim. 3:13). was no peace; .."

Eve eyed the fruit and saw that it was pleasing to the eye; she stared at it, meditated on it and then she took a bite. Samson saw Delilah, stared at her, meditated on her looks and had sex with her. Samson was driven by his lust. He saw her and desired her just like Eve saw the fruit and desired it. To desire something is to crave something or have an intense longing. His emotions and his body began to desire her. He began to crave her just like a person would crave ice cream. Whatever we open the door to or begin to feed becomes the object of our affections. This was the beginning of his soul being dominated, leading to his premature death.

I remember a young man announcing to me that he was going to enjoy breaking me down. Listen to those words. He said that he was going to have fun destroying my soul. Look at how a demonic spirit spoke through him and he commenced to doing so. He attempted to seduce and entice me with his words by occupying huge amounts of my time, talking to me for hours on end and then the chase ensued. He would disappear or suddenly become unavailable. Thanks be to God that this soul tie never became physical, but it did create substantial emotional and mental damage. A soul tie is most effective when the will of a person has been broken and they no longer have the power to resist. They can't say, "no". At that point, it's almost like the person is under a spell or in a trance. They're being controlled by a seducing spirit.

Delilah lied. She deceived Samson into believing that she only wanted to know the source of his anointing for love's sake. He believed that she was at peace with him, but the whole time he was sleeping with the enemy. Ezekiel 13:10 says, "Because, even because they have seduced my people, saying, Peace; and there was no peace…" Some men will promise that they come into your life to bring you peace. They may even declare that God sent them into your life. You may even insist that God sent this person into your life. In reality though, a seducing spirit is controlling you, deceiving and lying to you. When a seducing spirit is in operation, you become like a fool. You do foolish things, things that you regret. You regret the things you do because your choices lacked the wisdom of God. "The princes of Zoan are become fools, the princes of Noph are deceived; they have also seduced Egypt, even they that are the stay (cornerstone) of the tribes thereof. (Isaiah 19:13-14).

A cornerstone is an architectural term. A cornerstone is placed at the angle or corner of a building where two walls meet. Cornerstones are important in joining and binding the structure together. So even the strong Egyptian nobles were seduced and rendered powerless. The strong Samson was a cornerstone in God's army, but the mighty Samson fell due to a seducing spirit.

Samson had a spirit of lust inside of him and Delilah used a seducing spirit to connect to his spirit of lust. His sexual desire combined with Delilah's deceiving ways clouded his ability to discern the plot against his own life. "These things have I written unto you concerning them that seduce (try to deceive) you. But the anointing which ye have received of him abideth in you, and ye need not that any man teach you: but as the same anointing teacheth you of all things, and is truth, and is no lie, and even as it hath taught you, ye shall abide in him. (1 John 2:26-27). Delilah broke Samson down until she controlled his mind, will, body and emotions. The only thing that should break you is the word of God. A broken and contrite heart God will not despise (Psalm 51:17). This brokenness speaks of humility, not destruction.

God's desire is not to kill you, but to make you more mature and wise. "So, my dear brothers and sisters, you also died to the law through the body of Christ, that you might belong to another, to him who was raised from the dead, in order that we might bear fruit for God. For when we were in the realm of the flesh, the sinful passions aroused by the law were at work in us, so that we bore fruit for death. But now, by dying to what once bound us, we have been released from the law so that we serve in the new way of the Spirit, and not in the old way of the written code." (Romans7:4-6). You are no longer obligated to obey the lust of your flesh. You are no longer indebted or enslaved to sin if Christ has become your all in all.

What's in a name?
Delilah's name means coquette. A coquette is a flirt, a person who makes sexual overtures. The Hebrew meaning of the name Delilah is amorous, delight, languishing, temptress and night. Her name also means feeble or Philistine woman. Delilah helped Samson damage his soul, lose his anointing and eventually his life. In the biblical days, people didn't randomly name their children. Their names indicated their life's purpose. In like manner, Jews and Christians of this century give their children names according to their intended function or mission in the world. As we examine the relationship between Samson and Delilah, you will discover that she was used for the purpose for which she was named, however that does not negate the fact that Samson had free choice. Delilah used her seductive nature to entice Samson and he allowed himself to succumb to temptation. Her countrymen, the Philistines, agreed to give Delilah 1100 pieces of silver which is equivalent to about $704. Money is not evil, but the love of money is the root of all evil. (1 Tim. 6:10)

How Words Create a Soul Tie
Soul ties have certain things in common. The names, races and faces of the people you get into relationships with may be different, but the strategies are the same. You'll find that one of the ways that soul ties usually begin is with words. One or both of you communicate

with each other to express interest in each other. Afterwards, the conversation usually progresses into early morning and late night phone calls. It is during these times that most women bare their souls and many men lie to get what they want.

The man will typically find out what you like and tell you what you want to hear. He gains entrance into your heart through your ears. He uses flattering conversation to sway your heart. His silky words feed your imagination and if you take the bait, the soul tie begins. His words deceive your heart. "For they that are such serve not our Lord Jesus Christ, but their own belly; and by good words and fair speeches deceive the hearts of the simple" (Romans 16:18). His words are the bait and you bite on the bait that hides the hook.

Your Casanova may even hang on your every word. He is deeply attentive and acts as if he can't go a day without hearing your melodious voice. He may call you several times a day and engage in long conversations at night. He may even hint at you being wife material or may give you the nickname of "wifey". He monopolizes most of your time so that you can begin to think of him all of the time. He uses his words to draw you further into the relationship and create an emotional connection. Once an emotional bond is established, it is easier to twist and manipulate your soul.

The Role of Sex in a Soul Tie – Why the Enemy Wants You to Have Sex Outside of Marriage

A soul tie is strengthened with the passage of time, but the strongest strand of a soul tie is sex. It will bind and trap your soul. If you are not alert, the adversary will lure you into sex outside of marriage. At that point, you become a slave or prisoner of lust. Friends and family try to warn you against the relationship, but your soul is entangled and you ignore everyone. You even ignore your own conscience.

Sex is a powerful tool of expression that God created to be expressed between a man and a woman in holy matrimony. Marriage is honorable in all and the bed is undefiled (Heb. 13:4). When God instituted marriage, he also made sex as a component. God understood that sex expresses love, fellowship, and adoration between a husband and wife. Sex God's way is intended for procreation, recreation and communication. However, the enemy has corrupted sex. He wants you to engage in the sexual act outside of marriage so that you can sin against yourself and God (1 Cor. 6:18). Sex outside of marriage is sin against God and destroys the sanctity of sexual expression. Not to mention the fact that you introduce other variables like mistrust, unwanted pregnancies, disrespect and disease. If you and he can't control your sexual urges before marriage, what makes you think that you or he will be able to refrain from the temptation of adultery?

Samson was a Nazarite, set aside for God's purposes, but he had an appetite for women who did not worship Jehovah God, the God of Israel. His parents begged him to avoid relationships with strange women. They didn't want him to be unequally yoked, but Samson ignored them and allowed his body to control his actions.

In Judges 16:1, Samson travels to Gaza and as soon as he saw Delilah he had a sexual encounter with her. I can't emphasize enough that sex is one of the most powerful ways that the enemy uses to control your soul. Most soul ties have a sexual component. In fact, sex is usually the component that seals the soul tie. I want to reiterate that soul ties typically begin with a person using flattery to control your mind, will and emotions and sex makes the bond stronger. The man begins to manipulate you through your body. Now your body craves him and every time you engage in sex with him you form a stronger connection with sin, resulting in a stronghold. A stronghold is a fortress, barrier, garrison or tall wall erected for the specific purpose of keeping out enemies, but a stronghold can also make sure that nothing gets out. The person trapped in the prison is you. As you continuously yield to sin, it gets harder to resist.

Sometimes strongholds are created in our lives by other people through experiences like molestation, rape, incest or exposure to pornography. For instance, if a child is raised to believe that pornography is acceptable, a stronghold of perversion is being built in his/her life. Wrong thoughts about sex are built into that child's mind. If you continue to have sex outside of marriage, your body enjoys the pleasure and your mind imagines and longs for the next encounter, which builds a stronghold in your mind. Whoever or whatever you yield to becomes your master.

The bible says that we are to be filled with the spirit (Eph. 5:18) and sex is reserved for a husband and wife (Heb. 13:4). As you give more control of yourself to your flesh, your thoughts become murky. It's difficult to think objectively about the relationship when your body is experiencing intense enjoyment even though guilt and shame follow the sexual act outside of marriage. The guilt and shame is a natural response to grieving the holy spirit and violating God's commandments.

Arrogance
Pride comes before the fall (Prov. 16:18). In Judges 16:1, Samson sleeps with a prostitute named Delilah. In verse 3 of Proverbs, Samson uproots the gates of the city as a sign of his bravado. He was showing off his supernatural strength. Between verses 1 and 3, he never repents. He doesn't ask God for forgiveness for his sexual escapade. Remember, he was a Nazarite, anointed and chosen by God before birth. He did not marry Delilah, but he did sleep with her. Notice that between verses one and three he does not say, "Lord I'm sorry." He does not say, "Lord, help me." He does not say, "Lord, I'm struggling with my flesh." He is so cavalier. He's nonchalant. He laid with a prostitute, got up, demolished the city gates and continued with his normal routine of destroying the enemies of God. The problem is that he did not repent. Sin and ministry are not good companions. Be assured, that your sin will find you out (Num. 32:23).

In order for seduction to take place, there has to be an appeal to your senses, something you like. When tempted, no one should say,

"God is tempting me." For God cannot be tempted by evil, nor does he tempt anyone; but each person is tempted when they are dragged away by their own evil desire and enticed. Then, after desire has conceived, it gives birth to sin; and sin, when it is full-grown, gives birth to death (James 1:13-15).

Seduction is only appealing because it offers you something that promises to satisfy your urges. The serpent deceived Eve by making her think that the fruit is what she needed to be wise. Seduction overrides common sense and the Holy Ghost if you let it. She was already wise. The Father had made her. She was in the presence of God, living in His very presence. You see how the enemy deceives us. Then, he flattered her and told her that if she ate of it, it would make her wise.

In 2017, the conversation might go something like this. "God knows that we are made from the dust. He knows that you need sex. He made sex. It's okay. A little sex today won't hurt you. God is a forgiving God." After all, Adam and Eve didn't walk down the aisle of a church an express their wedding vows in front of a pastor. Sex is marriage. Why do we need a license? God knows we're human. The enemy incorporates some truth. While it is true that Adam and Eve did not walk down the aisle, it is also true that there was not another human being on the earth at that time besides them. God was their pastor. He officiated the ceremony. There is no authority higher than God. He did not need a representative because he was interacting with them directly. The bible says that "God knows we are made from dust (Psalm 103:14). In other words, he knows that we're human and subject to make mistakes. However, the bible also says that "a little leaven leaveneth the whole lump" (Gal. 5:9) and shall we continue in sin that grace may abound? God forbid. How shall we that are dead to sin, live any longer therein? (Rom. 6:1-2).

The enemy will magnify and twist the truth in order to appeal to your sensual nature, your bodily appetite, and soulish desires. He conveniently shines a spotlight on partial truth. The adversary doesn't have any new tricks, just new ways of presenting his schemes, but he will always come through the pride in one's lifestyle, the lust of the eyes or the lust of the flesh (1 John 2:16).

The devil will sweet talk you and make all kinds of promises to you, but he can't tell the truth and he can't keep promises. He only knows how to lie and deceive. That's what he does. Remember, his purpose is to steal you from purpose; to knock you out on the canvas so that you can never get back up again; to render you powerless during the time that you are supposed to be experiencing victory. He wants to distract you like he distracted Samson. That's his goal, but don't let him do that. Beat him at his own game with the word of God. See through his deception. Be discerning. God would not have us to be ignorant of the devil's devices (2 Cor. 2:11).

You don't have to swear off of men and please don't make wicked statements like, "All men are bad." That's not true. The power of life and death are in the tongue and you shall eat the fruit of your words (Prov. 18:21). Bless your life instead of cursing it. You can begin to pray, "Heavenly Father, I thank you for the man that you have for me, that our union was ordained by you and will be pleasing to you, fulfilling to us, make you smile and produce much fruit for the kingdom. I thank you that our marriage will be filled with Your love, joy, peace, wisdom, grace, passion, commitment, understanding, patience and self-control in Jesus' name. Amen.

However, be very alert because your adversary walks around like a roaring lion seeking whom he may devour (1 Pet. 5:8). Make sure that you discern the difference between a God-sent man and a counterfeit (See ch. 7) The counterfeit will be very close to God's best. The adversary's hallmark is lies and flattering words. If you have low-self-esteem, ask God to make the necessary adjustments in you so that you are not so desperate for approval and validation from a man. Realize that you are accepted by your Heavenly Father (Eph. 1:6). You are beautiful, valued, highly esteemed and treasured. (See affirmations in appendix.) The enemy deceived us in the past, but I speak in faith that you won't be tricked anymore. Deceivers will try to fool God's people, but they can't fool the elect (Matt 24:24).

Taking Your Cues From the World
Media defines success by the amount of your worldly possessions. How many times have we heard of famous or wealthy people who were very miserable? By now, we should have learned that money and material possessions don't guarantee happiness. In fact, money only accentuates who you are beneath the surface. If you were mean and selfish as a poor person, you'll be mean and selfish as a rich person. If you were generous as a poor person, you'll be a generous wealthy person.

We must stop taking our cues from the media and pop culture and begin to live by biblical principles and standards. What is the most important part of you according to the Word? It's the invisible part – your soul. Heaven and earth are passing away, but my word shall stand, saith the Lord (Matt. 24:35). Though my outer man (body) is perishing day by day, my spirit is getting stronger (2 Corinthians 4:16). Where ought our focus to be? Our focus ought to be on preparing ourselves for the return of the King.

The unwise virgins ran out of oil and were not ready for Christ's return (Matt. 25:7). Maybe they were at the mall, watching T.V., obsessed with their hair and looks. Personal care and beauty treatment has its place. Esther prepared herself for Ahaseurus, but even Esther came to a place where her spiritual convictions had to supersede her position as a queen. Her decision would determine the fate of an entire nation. She could not have been obsessed with make-up and clothes and still have made the right decision. In fact, she denied herself of food and water for three days so that she could make the right decision.

Deny worldly lifestyles and develop a work ethic. Ruth had a strong work ethic and Boaz noticed it. A real man of God will not only appreciate your natural beauty, but he will also be impressed with your work ethic and love for the Lord, your determination to stand upon the convictions of the Holy Spirit. Where is your faith and where is your focus? Do you want to be a woman of the world or a woman of faith? You can't serve two masters. You have to choose. That does not mean that you can't wear make-up or pants, but let everything be done in moderation and your identity must not be rooted in your looks or shape because what happens when either of those things change or fade? Then, where is your security? Your identity and security must be in Christ. We have taken on the status (state, attitude, mindset) of the world and that is why it is so difficult for us to find our identity.

Twenty-first century media is saturated with ungodly presentations and lust-filled shows and movies. Even today's commercials are very sensual. Even billboards utilize sexual imagery to sell their products. The cover page of magazines on the racks at the check-out counter feature scantily-clad women and bare-chested men. Lust is all around us and sometimes lust is on the inside of us.

The Lust In You
Lust is from the enemy. What is lust? It is an ungodly, intense longing for something; it's an out-of-control, disproportionate craving for someone or something. It is an inordinate desire. Inordinate means unusually or disproportionately large; excessive, unreasonable or extreme.

You can lust for wealth, fame and fortune. You can lust to be the center of attention at all times and do anything to get it. Lust means desire or passionate longing. It comes from the Greek workd, epithumia. Epithymia comes from epithumia. It means "focused on" and thymos means passionate desire. You are being lustful when you focus on satisfying your passionate desires even if it means offending God and grieving the Holy Spirit.

The fruit of the Spirit is the opposite of lust. According to Galatians 5:22 - 23, **"But the fruit of the Spirit is love, joy, peace, longsuffering, gentleness, goodness, faith, meekness, temperance: against such there is no law.** Temperance is self-control. We must be able to reign in our passions. Our desires should not control us; we should control our longings. That's why the bible tells us to crucify our flesh (Gal. 5:24) and part of the fruit of the Spirit is self-control (Gal. 5:22). A man must know how to possess his vessel. Lust pressures you. It was lust that made David's son rape Tamar and then after lust is conceived it produces more sin (James 1:15). After David's son violated Tamar, he tossed her aside.

His father also had a problem with lust. It was King David's lust that caused him to sin with Bathsheba. That sin led to more sin in the form of murder (2 Samuel 11:14). Sin begats sin. In order to cover his sin, David committed more sin. Soul ties will cause you to hide or attempt to hide, but what's done in the dark will come to light (Luke 8:17). That doesn't necessarily mean that you will be exposed in front of people, but what's more important is that your sin is open and revealed before God and your conscience will begin to bother you. Our conscience is a blessing from God. If it has not been seared, it lets us know when we've done something wrong.

Most children have a conscience. They know when they've done something wrong. No one has to tell them. Their conscience informs them. For instance, when mom tells her child to wait until after dinner to eat cookies. The child may wait until mom leaves the kitchen, and sneak a cookie or two. When mom returns to the kitchen and asks the toddler, "Did you eat a cookie?" The child will usually say, "No." Did mom teach that child how to lie? She didn't have to. We were all born in sin and shaped in iniquity, it's part of the fallen nature of mankind. The child knew that he had done something wrong.

Lust is disrespectful. It does not allow you to appreciate the person for who they are. Lust is one-thing focused. It causes you to focus on one aspect or feature while ignoring the rest. All Eve could see was that one apple, but she ignored all of the other beautiful trees that were at her disposal in the garden. Lust causes you to zoom in on one thing. Hollywood and the media are experts at stirring and feeding lust. The films, television movies, shows and commercials are saturated with lustful images and messages. Why do you think there is an inordinate focus on beauty and body? It is to feed and control the minds of the people so that they never pay attention to what really matters – their soul.

We should not assist this spirit by drawing attention to our breasts, behind, legs or overall shape. While we do not have to be dowdy, we do not need to dress provocatively or seductively. One of the definitions of provocative is to arouse sexual desire or interest, especially deliberately. The carnal mind is enmity against God (Rom. 8:7).

Lust must be conceived or birthed in the heart or mind (soul) before it can be acted on outwardly. It's an inside job. It's outcomes are ugly and can be deadly. You lust for a piece of chocolate or another piece of food. You imagine it in your mind and stare at images of food as they pop up on television commercials. You think for long periods of time about how good that food will be and then finally you agree with your thoughts and take action. YOU get up to find and purchase that food. That is the same process that is used before you engage in sexual sin. You have to focus on it, think about it, and imagine it, and build up an intense craving.

The lust of anything or anyone is ugly and gross. It distorts a person or thing's true value. It distorts a person's perception. A lustful person cannot be trusted because a lustful person will do or say anything to satisfy their desires. If unchecked, lust destroys everything it touches. It ruins marriages, friendships, trust and destinies. Lust is a strategy that the enemy has been using effectively throughout the centuries. The lust that I'm referring to is a misplaced desire. The energy that we use to consume our passions could be used on godly pursuits.

Some women find certain men hard to resist because they have muscles like Superman. But does he also have strong character? Is he a man of integrity? Samson was a strong, muscle-bound man who lacked integrity, which brought premature death. Society focuses on the external because Satan is the god of this world system. Casinos, whore houses, drugs, bars, strip clubs, money, and the fast food industry are built on the premise of lust. They offer convenient opportunities to get whatever you want. The enemy has designed these distractions so that you and I can focus and meditate on that one forbidden fruit. He increases your desire for the object of your passion so that you will sin. "Then desire when it has conceived gives birth to sin, and sin when it is fully grown brings forth death" (James 1:15).

Most of the movies, music and entertainment of this world is designed to draw you away from God. When the devil was kicked out of heaven, he set out on a massive campaign to destroy and pervert everything that God created – starting with mankind, God's prized creation. "What is man that thou art mindful of him? and the son of man, that thou visitest him? For thou hast made him a little lower than the angels, and hast crowned him with glory and honour. Thou hast made him a little lower than the angels" (Psalm 8:4-6).

Some women lust to become the wife of a minister, not knowing the requirements. You'll need more than a pretty face, hat and dress to occupy that position. To hold that position with honor, you must be a praying woman, a virtuous woman, a compassionate woman, a slow-to-anger woman, a gracious host, a generous woman and the list goes on an on.

A man shouldn't lust after his wife in an ungodly way because that means that she becomes a sex toy or object. She is reduced to a body with no concern for her feelings or opinions instead of being valued as a human being. You can spot a woman who values herself. A woman who values herself is not easily persuaded. She doesn't always have to be vocal. She thinks before she speaks. She is considerate of others. She is not easily approached. She asks a lot of questions. She listens more than she speaks.

Once you realize how precious you are to your Heavenly Father and all of the trouble He went through to reconcile you back to Him, you will never allow another man to devalue or degrade you. Never! You teach people how to treat you by how you present yourself. Your husband-to-be must know that you are not a toy. He can't just pick you up and put you down at his convenience. You are a child of the King (Ps. 45:13). You are the Father's daughter. You are his choicest wine from his choicest vine.

You show people how to treat you by your actions, by what you tolerate or refuse, by the boundaries that you draw, by the stand that you take. No one can walk in and out of your life unless you allow it. You are chosen for a set time and a set purpose. Ask the Lord to teach you how to use your time wisely to fulfill His purpose for your life. Psalm 90:12 says, "Teach us how to number our days, that we may gain a heart of wisdom."

You are not to be neglected, abandoned, tossed aside or thrown onto the trash heap. That's unacceptable. It is not an option. Your God-man will rise to the level of expectation and offer the respect that a queen deserves. He, in his priestly garments, will arise and take you as his queen. There will be a oneness and an understanding that permeates the relationship. Do not participate in a one-sided relationship. You should not be the one who is always giving, always listening or always available. He must be sacrificial as well. You should not be the person who is always waiting by the phone, hoping and praying that he will respond to the affection that you have displayed. No! No! No! You are far too valuable and far too precious to be left hanging, wondering and searching.

The Lord validates Himself, proves who He is, by guarding your heart, protecting you, and never leaving you (Deut. 31:6; Heb. 13:5). Your future mate should also have the same ability to love you like Christ (Eph. 5:25). Recognizing your value, trusting in your Heavenly Father and speaking the word over your life does not mean that the enemy will not try to entice you to sin. He will try, but you must learn to submit your passions to God and resist the devil (James 4:7).

On the other hand, a husband should have a passionate desire for his wife in a "Song of Solomon" way, but that's in addition to loving and cherishing her as a whole person. God is not a kill-joy; he is the

Creator and Master of all things good. "Every good and perfect gift cometh down from the Father of Lights with whom there is no variableness nor shadow of turning" (James 1:17).

Hook-ups must be divine in nature. We have to return to God's way of doing, being and thinking, and believing. We need a mind change because most of our minds have been poisoned by a worldly view fed by media (news, television shows, movies, music, social media, billboards, radio commercials, etc.). We have to renew our minds.

If you've been born again, your body actually is the temple of the Lord. God lives and resides there and should be honored, respected, treasured, valued and highly esteemed for occupying your body and only one man deserves to go into your holies of holies – your husband. Believers have messed up because we have adopted worldly views. Lust drives you while love leads you.

Lust must be cast out through confession and repentance and then it must be forsaken. You lust for his biceps, but you detest his personality. He lusts for your body, but he hates it when you speak.

A Godly Woman's Standard
You must teach men who you are and how you are to be treated. That is a lesson that only you can teach. You teach a man how to teach you through your actions. My motto is I can show you better than I can tell you. A man must know from the beginning that you are a woman with standards. Why are you disquieted or afraid? Hope thou in God for I shall yet praise Him who is the health of my countenance (Ps. 42:11). Amen.

Don't worry. Worry is not of God. Whatever is not of faith is sin. Know that God has a perfect plan for you. He will supply ALL of your need (inclusive of the plurality) according to His riches in glory in Christ Jesus (Phil. 4:19) so be joyful. Be contented. Be in expectation while resting in Him. Rejoice in Him who revives your soul and refreshes your spirit. Be whole. Be joyful. Be complete. Be at peace.

6
Man Traps

THERE ARE SEVERAL traps that men set for women. By nature, men are hunters. They enjoy the chase. Unfortunately, sin has perverted the natural inclination of men to pursue women. Far too many men, have decided to manipulate the emotions of women by playing certain games with their minds.

The Wife Game
A man may try to gain benefits from you by turning you into his "wife". If you are dating him, you are not his wife no matter how many times he calls you "wifey" or tells you that he will marry you. Even if you are wearing a wedding ring and the wedding date has been set, you are not his wife yet. Please beware of manipulation. He should not be requiring things of you as if you are his wife. You should not be washing his clothes, shopping for his groceries or dropping off his dry cleaning.

We must be wise enough to recognize when abuse is occurring. You are not a dumpster or a trash bag and even when you get married, you are still not a garbage can. If he has a host of problems and unresolved issues, let him talk to his therapist, seek the Lord, get a mentor and/or accountability partner(s) and draw strength from the word of God. Unless you are a therapist or a trained counselor, why go down that path and risk developing a soul tie that will hurt you in the end? Remember, the way you begin a relationship is how it will continue.

Begin to draw boundaries and shut the door to any attempt at abuse or misuse of your emotions, will and thoughts. Let the man you're interested in, get healed. Otherwise, he will simply bring his pain to you. He will add pain to your life instead of purpose, passion and pleasure. Multiplication and addition takes place when a man and a woman come together. Either heartache or joy will be added to your life. You decide.

There is a reason that the man's sexual organ is outward and ours is inward. The man imparts and plants the seed. Whatever is in that man will be planted into you physically and spiritually. A wife is generally a reflection of her husband. That is why it is so important to consider if you like the qualities of the man you are dating? Would you be happy taking on his characteristics?

You also need to make sure that you are not unequally yoked. I don't only refer to the obvious meaning of a saved person marrying an unbeliever. I am also referring to two believers who are not meant for each other. They're both saved, but she's been saved for more than a decade and she has continued to grow in the things of God while the man she met is satisfied with going to bible study and Sunday morning worship. He does not want any greater revelation from God. He is fine with being a nominal Christian. You two are unequally yoked. If you marry him, you will soon become angry that he does not desire to know Christ deeply and he will become frustrated with you as you nag him to fast, pray and intercede more.

You want to make sure that a man is adding and multiplying the right things. This man should help you subtract negativity while adding and multiplying joy, truth, peace, love, wisdom and purpose. He should be like an oasis, providing refreshment and a different outlook that helps you appreciate the provision and vastness of God. No one is perfect, but God will grace both of you to handle the difficult or challenging moments of your life because when you were single you took the time to involve God in your daily life.

You should not be playing or acting as the Holy Spirit (helper) to a man that is not or your husband. Why are you being "wife" to someone who is not your husband? Why are you trying to prove what a good woman you are to a man who is not yours? That's the trick of the enemy. Stop!!! Pour all of that oil on Jesus. Praise Him. He will accept your praise, sacrifice and obedience. Love Him first. Love Him with all of your heart, soul, mind and strength. After all, doesn't he deserve that? Doesn't he deserve first place? Don't be afraid. Give Him first place. He deserves it. Let Him heal your heart. Let him drench your heart with adoration for Him, forgiveness for all those who hurt you and forgiveness for yourself. You are His chosen, his beloved, his sweet one, the one who brings Him joy, the one He loves to commune with. Let Him be all that He wants to be to you. Don't be afraid. Enter in. He is your Abba Father. He will not hurt you. Let Him heal those wounds, insecurities and shortcomings. Let no one separate you from the love of the Father. Will you trust the Lord with every aspect of your life? Will you trust Him with the beginning, middle and end? Will you surrender to His will for your life?

The Substitution Game
Sometimes you miss having someone to be with. It's not that you liked the person. You liked the company that they provided; they were a good substitute. Often soul ties are formed because of what I call the substitution game. Basically, you settle for a person to avoid being alone. This game is common among divorced men or men who are fresh out of a relationship. Often times, they will immediately begin dating someone right after a break-up or quickly remarry after a divorce. She may not be the woman that he really wants to be with, but he will substitute her for the woman he really longs to be with. He will attach himself to someone who will keep him distracted. Women also play the substitution game for the same reason.

The benefit of dating a substitute is the emotional satisfaction of companionship without having to make a commitment. In the meantime, the substitute may be shortchanged if he/she is ready and wants to receive the fullness of all that a healthy God-ordained relationship entails. If you settle for being a substitute, you will be cheated out of a genuine relationship because the man will use you for his personal convenience. He drains the life and vitality out of the substitute, sucking away her bone and marrow, that which was ordained for her future spouse. So we must not play the substitution game no matter how lonely we get. It is unfair to you and the other person. Both people are being cheated out of a healthy relationship.

Build-a-Woman
Beware of the man who has decided that he will build a woman and you will be his guinea pig. He sets out to change everything about you little by little or all at once. Either way, this man does not like you at all. He is also a person who lives in a fantasy world and you should leave him alone with his fantasy. This man does not appreciate the unique beauty that is you.

You are fearfully and wonderfully made (Psalm 139:14). You were created by God. You are his handiwork (Ephesians 2:10). This man is not the potter. Who gave him the authority to destroy your DNA - everything that makes you who you are? Never allow anyone to desecrate what God has created. If he is offering healthy suggestions, that's different. However, if there are several things about you that he doesn't like and he sets out to remake you, you might want to let him go. There's probably a longer list of things he doesn't like about you. He just hasn't shared his list yet. If he starts pointing out a lot of things, you either haven't done the needed examination and work on yourself or he just wishes you were someone else.

Assignment or Potential Mate?
You have to fill your cup and his cup too. The relationship is one-sided. You're always pouring into him. He's always taking from you and never replenishing the withdrawal. That is not a relationship. It may be an assignment, but assignments have to be kept in their place.

An assignment is a person who God has allowed to gain access to your life for the purpose of helping them in a particular area. Maybe this man was brought into your life so that you could point him to Christ by your godly character. Maybe you are supposed to be like a sister to him. Ask God for clarity. Distinguish an assignment from a potential mate. Separate your assignment from your heart. A person can be an assignment and not be your soul mate. Know the difference. Don't mix the two and don't allow anyone to blur the lines or cross the boundaries. They must never be given access as if it is a romantic relationship or courtship.

Assignments have to know that they are assignments and restricted to a certain area of your life. You must establish boundaries. They don't have the right to bleed over into your personal space except in intercessory prayer. You must draw those boundaries. Sometimes, God assigns someone that we are to pray for, counsel and/or be a sounding board for, but we must not blur the lines. Assignments aren't necessarily friends. Friends are able to reciprocate and do reciprocate and want to reciprocate. Assignments usually need you to pour into them.

Jesus is the rescuer and He will use you as a vessel, but don't confuse your help or intercession with the role of Christ the mediator. That is a sure and easy way to be misaligned, misplaced and in the wrong space in your heart, doing the wrong thing at the wrong time with right intentions. An assignment can become a mate, but you would definitely have to know that God willed that for your life.

7
The Masquerade

EVIL SPIRITS LOVE to masquerade and camouflage themselves so that you are never aware of their presence or influence upon a person or situation. For instance, lust often masquerades as love. A love for someone's anointing can perpetrate as a love for the person. A man can seem like your potential mate, but he's really a distraction from the enemy or a platonic assignment from God. This is where discernment kicks in. We must be able to distinguish the real from the fake. Apostle Paul warned us that in the last days there would be deceivers (2 Tim. 3:13).

Remember that magnet that I talked about. You took a rope and tied it around your own heart, but you just didn't know it. You were under a spell. Your soul was manipulated by lust, fantasy and denial. It could be the lust in him and the lust in you. You two enjoyed sex with each other. You fantasized about meeting someone you could share your world with and you thought he was the one or you knew that he wasn't the one, but you pretended that he was the one so that you wouldn't have to be alone.

Is it love or lust?
Love gives while lust takes. Love gives the best, hopes for the best, wants the best for you, seeks the best for you, is concerned about

your success and well-being. Love is not selfish, rude, demanding, boastful, self-seeking, self-willed or impatient. Love is patient, self-sacrificing, humble, kind, gentle, long-suffering, full of good fruit, easy to be entreated, forgiving, hopeful, believes all things, endures all things (Gal. 5:22).

Lust is selfish, rude, boastful, seeks to satisfy the flesh at any cost; will lie, compromise, deny the truth to get what it wants. Lust is self-focused; will always seek to satisfy itself first. "Whatever is born of the flesh is flesh, but what is born of the Spirit is life everlasting" (John 3:6). "If you sow to the Spirit you will reap life, but if you sow to the flesh, you will reap corruption." (Gal. 6:8) How do you know if it is lust or love? Ask yourself these questions:

> Has my association with this person made me a better person?
>
> Has it drawn me closer to the Lord or pushed me further away?
>
> Has it enhanced my prayer life and worship time or has it decreased?
>
> Am I having sex with this person even though I am not married to him?
>
> Have I found myself compromising my values and beliefs in order to please this person?
>
> Do I avoid introducing this person to family and friends because I have a guilty conscience?
>
> Do I hide this person from family and friends because deep down I know this relationship isn't right?

Can you say that the Lord is pleased with this relationship and how you are carrying it out?

Have you done things that you are ashamed of and is that the pattern lately with this person?

Do you all have anything in common other than physical attraction?

Is he of the same faith?

Judges 16:4 says that Samson loved Delilah. Was it love or was it lust? Lust can imitate love. There was no indication of God's involvement in their relationship. Contrast their bond to the relationships of Adam and Eve, Rebecca and Isaac, Ruth and Boaz, Ahaseurus and Esther. You can see that God was involved in their unions. God made Eve for Adam. He was their personal matchmaker. "And the Lord God caused a deep sleep to fall upon Adam, and he slept: and he took one of his ribs, and closed up the flesh instead thereof; And the rib, which the Lord God had taken from man, made he a woman, and brought her unto the man" (Gen. 2:21-22).

Abraham prayed for his servant to find a godly companion for his son, Isaac. "The Lord God of heaven, which took me from my father's house, and from the land of my kindred, and which spake unto me, and that sware unto me, saying, Unto my seed will I give this land; he shall send his angel before thee, and thou shalt take a wife unto my son from thence." (Gen. 24:7) God answered his prayer. Even Abraham's servant prayed to God for help in finding a wife for Isaac. "And he said O Lord God of my master Abraham, I pray thee, send me good speed this day, and shew kindness unto my master Abraham" (Gen. 24:12). He continued his prayer in verse 14 with, "And let it come to pass, that the damsel to whom I shall say, Let down thy pitcher, I pray thee, that I may drink; and she shall say, Drink, and I will give thy camels drink also: let the same be she that thou hast appointed for thy servant Isaac: and thereby shall I know that thou hast shewed kindness unto my master." (Gen. 24:14).

Naomi acted as a type of Holy Spirit when she advised Ruth how to present herself to Boaz (Ruth 3:3-4). When Boaz was supervising his field, he took note of Ruth's character. He knew that Ruth's husband had died and he observed how Ruth had taken care of her mother-in-law as if Naomi was her mother. Notice how he was impressed with more than her physical appearance. Their union produced a godly lineage from which King David was born and eventually the Messiah.

Similarly, it was in God's divine plan that Esther meet Ahasuerus. Esther's position as the wife of a powerful king was God-ordained (Eph. 4:14). Through her the Jews were saved from the destructive plan of one of the king's advisors. "Then the king Ahasuerus said unto Esther the queen and to Mordecai the Jew, Behold, I have given Esther the house of Hama, and him they hanged upon the gallows, because he laid his hand upon the Jews" (Gen. 8:7). There is evidence of God's involvement in their relationships. The same cannot be said of Samson and Delilah. Your union must be purposeful. God must approve of it.

Samson and Delilah's connection was superficial. Although Delilah was a ploy set up by the Philistines to entrap Samson, Samson was a willing participant. As soon as he saw her, he had a sexual relationship with her and by verse three he's feeling like he loves the woman. Sex can trick your mind. You can think you love someone, when in fact you don't really love them, you "lust them". It is the feeling of satisfaction, the emotional high and the physical arousal that can perpetrate as love. Since Samson thought that he loved her, his thoughts made the soul tie stronger. The spirit of seduction entered his mind and distorted his perception.

Please understand that the enemy does not love you or me. He only has his interest at heart. He is totally selfish, a liar and consumed with jealousy. He wants to be like the most high God, but since he can't be God, he does the next best thing. He goes about every day seeking to destroy God's creation. What is his incentive for going after humans? Very simple. We are made in God's image and likeness (Gen. 1:26). Not only does the devil hate God, but he hates anything like God. Therefore, he hates you and me. His mission day and night is to get you to fall away from God. What better way to do that than to manipulate your soul? He wants you to be so confused that you don't know whether you're coming or going. Samson was distracted by his flesh. Lust perpetrated as love while the enemy was plotting to end his life and ministry.

Samson is consumed with lust and the enemy uses Samson's misplaced focus to distract him from his assignment as a man of God. When you or I don't dwell in the secret place of the most High God (Psalms 91), we are exposed and susceptible to the schemes of the enemy. The enemy of our souls looks for an entry point, a way to access our mind. That's why the bible says give no place to the devil. (Eph. 4:27). When the enemy found an opening in Samson's armor I can imagine him saying to himself, "Aha, Samson is exposed. Now I can kill him". The devil goes for the jugular. He wants to eliminate every trace of Samson so that his existence can become a memory.

Not only does the enemy want to kill you mentally, emotionally, and spiritually. He also wants to physically annihilate you; wipe out any trace or memory of you. Why would the adversary go through so much trouble? If the enemy can sidetrack you, then the people you are assigned to or the tasks that you were supposed to complete for the kingdom of God will not get done by you. How disappointing would it be to meet Jesus in heaven and not be able to cast crowns before his feet because you allowed yourself to be distracted?! The enemy used lust to minimize Samson's effectiveness.

Samson tied a rope around his own heart. His soul was manipulated by lust, fantasy and denial. Maybe you've fantasized about meeting someone you could share your life with and you thought he was the one or you knew that he wasn't the one, but you pretended that he was so that you wouldn't have to be alone. Deception has so many faces. Below are some more examples of counterfeit love.

More Deception
Attracted to Your Anointing Doesn't Mean They're Attracted to You. A person is amazed by your preaching and musical ability. They may even get great joy, relief, healing and deliverance from your preaching and singing, but that alone is not enough of a reason to pursue a relationship. You and your anointing are not the same. They can be attracted to your anointing, but hate your personality, style of dress and sense of humor. You can't sing, preach, and prophesy 24 hours a day. They must love the person that you are even when you are not doing ministry work or expressing your gifts, talents and abilities. They must be genuinely attracted to who you are as a person.

A Good Listener. You are a good listener or he is a good listener. Everyone tells you you're a good listener, male and female, strangers, acquaintances and friends. Are you going to marry everyone who compliments you for your listening skills? How much more ridiculous is it to marry someone solely because he says you're a good listener.

Projects & Counterfeit Suitors. I can't count the number of times that I took on projects. He was immature, wounded and dangerous and I was immature, wounded and dangerous. What made both of us dangerous was that we were not mature enough to help each other so we added more damage, confusion, frustration and strife to each other's souls.

What is a project? A project is something that requires fixing. Ever since I was a little child, I seemed to have had a knack for attracting projects – people who were broken and needed to be fixed. This became a pattern for me. I realized that many of the men that I dated needed fixing so I became their mother. I began to raise them. That is wrong and backwards! Who raises up men? God and other godly men. Even the most excellent mother still needs the influence of a positive man to help raise a boy. Fathers are supposed to instruct their male children in godliness. It was never intended that the woman alone would have to raise a godly male seed.

Raising a man in a relationship is very exhausting. It's exhausting because you are taking on a role that was never intended for you. The bible says that the man is the head of the woman and Christ is the head of the man (1 Corinthians 11:3). Don't be blindsided. Stop the madness before it starts. Recognize the red flags.

8
Red Flags

RED FLAGS SYMBOLIZE warning or danger. Red flags are raised during certain sporting events, on ships and for traffic control signaling potential trouble ahead. Often times, people's actions raise red flags, but we tend to ignore them for whatever reason(s). We rationalize that things will change or that it's only a small flaw. Red flags make you uncomfortable. Even if you sense discomfort for a moment, don't ignore that feeling. I became an expert at fooling myself until I learned that those gnawing feelings are usually an indication of a deeper problem. Recognize that feeling and monitor the frequency of it.

Your intuition signals that something is wrong. The holy spirit prompts us. Take notice. Some red flags are subtle while others scream, "Stop!" They usually repeat themselves. For instance, he loses his temper quickly over little things. Perhaps you make an innocent comment and he becomes very angry. You start to notice that his angry outbursts and rude comments are a recurring pattern. He may make a sarcastic comment about everything and everyone, including you. Frequent sarcasm is usually an indication of insecurity, a pessimistic outlook, a general dissatisfaction with life or a covering used as an opportunity to insult you and others. Red flags are indicators of larger problems. Don't ignore them. Save yourself from future problems. This is not a call to paranoia, but it is a call to discernment. Your soul is valuable and you should not be careless with it.

Red Flag #1 - Arrogance
It's all about him. The conversations begin and end with him. Warning! Warning! Warning! When a man can only speak about himself, how good he looks, how many people complimented him today, and how wonderful he is, beware! That is an indication that he is self-centered or insecure. Either way, you need to watch out. They're both extremes. So where will you fit in? Will there be competition? Will he become insecure if someone looks at you or compliments you? Will he become jealous of you or the attention you receive? Will he feel that all eyes should be on him and all compliments should be given to him?

Will he even have the desire, capacity, and/or ability to cultivate you or will he be so concerned with himself to the point that you could spiritually bleed to death and he wouldn't notice it? That's why character is so important. Samson was full of pride. He slept with a prostitute and didn't bother to ask God for forgiveness.

The outside of a person does not necessarily reveal the inner workings of the person. Samson had superhuman strength given to him by God. He was probably a very muscular man, but his character was weak. Be concerned about the character of the man you're dating or interested in. What is his character like? Does he keep his word? Does he apologize when he makes a mistake? Is he interested in you as a person? Your well-being? Your desires? Your wants? Your plans?

Red Flag # 2 – Your body controls your decisions.
As soon as Samson saw Delilah, he slept with her (Judges 16:1). Is lust the primary attraction to the man you like? In other words, is his physical appearance the main reason you want to be with him? Do you know enough about his habits, history, family background, or goals? Or maybe you know a lot about him, but his lifestyle is incompatible

with yours. Nevertheless, you are captivated by his swag, his chiseled body, his handsome face, his charming ways and stylish clothes.

The bible says that as soon as Samson laid eyes on Delilah, he slept with her. There was no conversation at all. Who was this woman? He didn't know anything about her except that he was physically attracted to her. The bible doesn't record that Samson prayed and asked God anything about her. He just allowed his flesh to rule. You may say that Samson's attraction was the same as Isaac's attraction to Rebecca or Jacob's attraction to Rachel, but that's not true. Isaac was looking for a wife and the bible reveals that Rebecca's character had been observed. She was an honorable woman. The bible records that she was beautiful, but that wasn't the only characteristic that she possessed. A relationship that is solely built on looks won't endure challenges that require strong character or integrity. The bible describes Rachel as a beautiful woman, but Jacob did not sleep with her until he married her. In fact, he waited for 14 years before he married her. A man should be willing to sacrifice for you. If he is not willing to sacrifice for you, you must question how much he really loves you. If he wants to sleep with you as soon as he meets you, you need to refuse that offer. A man should respect and honor you enough to delay his own desires.

Red Flag # 3 – Nothing in Common!
What did Samson and Delilah have in common? Sex. What do you have in common with the man that you're with or interested in? Maybe he is in full-time ministry, but you can't stand the thought of being in full-time ministry or he loves the corporate world, but you're in full-time ministry and he only wants limited involvement with working for the Lord. How can two walk together except they agree? (Amos 3:3). You can't have sex all of the time (and you shouldn't be having it unless you are married). At some point, you must leave the bedroom. Then what? What will you talk about? What will you laugh about? You should enjoy each other's company before sex in marriage. A man should be able to turn you on by the way he treats you, by his

kindness, tenderness, concern, strong character, high level of responsibility and attention to your needs. In the same way, you should be a woman of noble character, a virtuous woman without a spotty reputation. Don't lower your standards. Don't give him the rights and privileges that only an honorable man who marries you is entitled to.

Red Flag #4 – Tell Me All Of Your Secrets
A soul tie blinds you to red flags. Delilah asked Samson, " Where does your strength come from?" (Judges 16:6) That was nothing but the devil. She just met this man and that's the first thing she asks him. She didn't even ask him, "How was your day?" She could have asked him, "How many battles did you win today?" Instead, she wants to know the source of his anointing so that he can be destroyed. And that's what the enemy wants to do to you. He wants to rob you of your anointing. Sometimes your "boo" is being used by the enemy to destroy you or your ministry. He may be unaware that he is a tool in the enemy's hand or he may be dating you for his own personal gain. Either way, you will suffer negative effects from a soul tie. Whether he's aware of the enemy is not your concern. You just need to run from such men to preserve your life.

By the way, the enemy will sometimes use men in your church or men at work or in your neighborhood who claim to love the Lord. Just because he regularly attends church does not mean that the church is in him. If I married or dated every man who said that God told him that I am his wife, I would be a messed up woman. Not everyone who says, "Lord, Lord...." belongs to God. (Matt. 7:21-23) Some women say, but he's a pastor, he's a minister of music, he's a deacon, he's a Sunday school teacher. So what? A title is not synonymous with godly character. Maybe he has the best intentions, but he's not delivered and he's struggling with pride, pornography, homosexuality or some other sin. Look beyond the title and ask God for discernment.

When you meet a man and he wants to know your deepest secrets right away, something is wrong. When a man meets you and he immediately wants to know everything about you, that's a red flag. This actually happened to me a couple of times. Each man had the same approach. One was a little more experienced than the other so he surrounded his questions with a lot of flattery. He would give me a long list of compliments then sneak in a question. He would continue with this pattern hoping to gain control of my soul. I'd like to point out that he had a lot of good qualities, but he had learned to operate this way to protect himself from hurt. The sad revelation about a person who operates like this is that the individual doesn't realize that he needs to be delivered from the pain of his past. In the end, he only hurts himself and others because he can never experience the joy of vulnerability with another soul until he releases his fears and pain to God.

Each one of the guys I mentioned in the previous paragraph asked me a multitude of personal questions right away. One of them bombarded me with a long list of questions including "Do you have any children?" "Have you been married before?" "Do you plan on getting married?" "What were you like in junior high school?" "What were you like in elementary school?" "Did you graduate from high school?" "What are your future plans?"

Anytime you meet someone and they want to know everything about you from A-to-Z right away, the person usually has a hidden agenda. What's the rush? You want to ask the person, "Do you have some plans that I don't know about? Is there some scheme that you're trying to execute?" "A secret mission that you want to carry out, like Delilah did?" "Why do you need to know so much so soon?" Whenever someone has an alterior motive, such as to seduce you into sex outside of marriage, to destroy your ministry, to diminish your anointing, to get a green card so they can stay in the country, they will usually be in a rush. That's why you must not rush. I don't care how good a man looks, how anointed, intelligent, gentle, courteous or harmless he may appear to be. "Wait, I say on the Lord and be of good courage. And he will strengthen your heart" (Ps. 27:14).

The role of the holy spirit is critical. The holy spirit will lead and guide you into all truth (John 16:13). He will reveal what is hidden

(Heb. 4:13). It is important to be able to discern the real from the fake. Counterfeit money works because it's so close to authentic bills, but a closer examination will reveal the phoniness. It's the same way with men. The Holy Spirit will reveal what is true about a person and how much you should reveal. My mother taught me never to tell a man everything about myself right away and even if he is safe, you still can tell him EVERYTHING. There are some things that should be left between you and God.

Judges 16:6 is a glaring red flag. Delilah boldly asks Samson for the source of his strength. She says, "Tell me, I pray thee, wherein thy great strength lieth…" In other words, she wants to know the source of his anointing, the source of his power. This is a clear sign that she is not of God. If she were serving Samson's God she would know that Yahweh is the source of his power, but she wanted even more intimate details. She wanted to know about the Nazarite vows; what the angels had told his mother.

How did she know to even ask him that question? She had been hired by the Philistines to seduce him so that he would reveal the details of his Nazarite consecration (Judges 13:4-5). The devil has also hired men to seduce you, to uncover your secrets. He has hired men to gain your trust and then manipulate your emotions to their benefit. All men aren't evil, but some men will bring evil into your life if you allow it, but you can guard yourself against that travesty. Recognize a player when he comes. He'll immediately try to gain access to all of your past, all of your hurts and disappointments so that he can portray himself as the opposite kind of guy, thereby winning your trust and setting you up for a fall. We must also deal with the lust in our own souls. The bible says, "Let no man say when he is tempted, I am tempted of God: for God cannot be tempted with evil, neither tempteth he any man: But every man is tempted, when he is drawn away of his own lust, and enticed (James 1:13-14).

Delilah wanted to know how Samson was able to beat animals and men with his bare hands. She was paid to find out how to end his effectiveness in ministry. Some men have been hired by the enemy to end your ministry or to stop it before it begins. They've been hired to keep you hurt and wounded, to keep you occupied with Mr. Wrong so that you never meet Mr. Right. The Philistines wanted to stop the power that flowed through Samson. The men of her culture hated him. He had defeated the Philistines over and over again. He had been a formidable opponent, showcasing the power of Jehovah God. They wanted to kill his ministry. What does Delilah get out of it? Money. What does Samson get out of his association with Delilah? Death.

Red Flag #5 – How can I hurt you?
Judges 16:6 says, **"...**and wherewith thou mightiest be bound to afflict thee." Delilah asks Samson how she can afflict him. According to Strong's Concordance, the Hebrew meaning of "afflict" has several definitions including "to look down or browbeat; to depress literally or figuratively, deal harshly with, hurt, ravish and weaken." Delilah wanted to deeply wound Samson. She wanted to weaken his anointing and bring him pain.

Who in their right mind would stay with someone who is trying to bring hurt or pain? A soul tie makes your brain turn to mush. The sexual satisfaction overrules your logic. Samson closed his eyes to the devilish side of Delilah. She asked him three times how she could end his ministry (Judges 16: 6, 10, 13, 15). Verse 16 says after she asked him four times, she pressed him daily. Come on Samson, wake up! Soul ties poke out your spiritual eyes so that you can't see clearly.

Losing one's anointing or experiencing a significant decrease of anointing is one of the greatest pains of a believer. A diminishing of anointing is painful because you compare how you used to be to how you are and you begin to feel shame and disgust as you reflect on your new condition. Separation from God is painful. Adam and Eve knew this feeling all too well. For them, there was a diminished relationship with the Father, a death in the garden, a separation. Samson was getting further and further away from the will of God. We must be careful about who we allow to influence us. Adam was married, but he allowed Eve to influence his decision. He yielded to Eve. Likewise, Samson chose to expose himself to Delilah, a woman who did not know, respect or love Yahweh, Jehovah God. Why couldn't Samson hear her death wish? Soul ties diminish your discernment because your focus is no longer on pleasing God. Your focus has shifted to pleasing yourself. Just as Eve's focus had shifted from pleasing God to pleasing herself. Adam's focus shifted to pleasing his wife with a disregard for what God had commanded.

Delilah asked Samson, "How can I bring pain to you?" (Judges 16:10). Why would you want to be around someone who's asking you how they can harm you? That's a major red flag and yet many of us have settled for this kind of interaction just so that we can say we have someone or avoid being alone. What a steep price to pay! We get involved in soul ties only to find out that the person did not have our best interest at heart. Samson lied to Delilah. The problem with this is that he's playing with the devil.

The devil is an ancient foe. He was here before you and I so he knows all of the tricks. The enemy tried to tempt Jesus when he was fasting for forty day. Therefore, we are no match for the devil without the Lord Jesus Christ on our side. We need the strength of God and the wisdom of God. Don't play with the devil. Once you realize it's the devil, back up! Samson was enjoying entertaining Delilah with his lies. She repeatedly asked him how she could hurt him and he would make up some lie. He was having fun, but Delilah was ruthless. He didn't know that she was setting him up for a fall. He was extremely confident in his ability to keep the game going but once again pride comes before the fall (Prov. 16:18). Delilah didn't know that he was lying so she believed his story and attempted to bind him.

Red Flag # 6 – When A Person Shows You Who They Are, Believe Them
So Samson tells Delilah a lie, but she thinks it's the truth. She uses information that he told her privately against him. Each time she sent men to kill Samson based on the fake information he gave her,

she was revealing her personality. She betrays his confidence. How do you recognize this red flag? It usually occurs when you share a secret with him and he uses the information to hurt you. Run for the hills!

At this point in the soul tie, Samson is so blinded by his lust and the sexual encounter that he doesn't realize that Delilah is setting him up for a fall. He is blinded to the reality of what's really going on. By the way, Delilah doesn't have to be a woman. Delilah can be a man. Delilah is a seductive spirit. Most soul ties involve some form of seduction.

Red Flag # 7 – I'll Beg If I Have To
In Judges 16:13, Delilah makes demands and begs Samson to tell her how she can hurt him. She starts whining. She begs Samson several times to reveal his secrets. Scripture says that a man would rather dwell in the corner of a rooftop than in a house with a cantankerous woman (Prov. 25:24). She wants him to tell her how she can stop him from being anointed. Most men will not be as obvious as Delilah by making direct requests. Whether the man is direct or indirect about his desire, the purpose of the enemy is the same. He wants to dry up your anointing.

As I read the conversations between Samson and Delilah I kept asking myself, "Why does he stay with a woman who wants to know how she can hurt him?" I'm sure we've asked the same question about other people where we could see that the relationship had turned sour. To us it's so obvious. But when you're in the middle of a soul tie, it's not obvious that you're being deceived. That's why I wrote this book. I don't want you to be deceived anymore. Learn the signs so that you don't waste your time committing to someone who will bring you down, tarnish your reputation and possibly cause premature death.

A soul tie covers your eyes so that you can't see the truth. That's why soul ties can be so dangerous. You don't even know you're being set up. And because the sexual encounters that they had were apparently so pleasing at the moment that it blocked out all rationale. All of his reasoning ability just went out of the window. In verse 11, Samson continues to play with Delilah and pretends to tell her the secret to his anointing. He lies to her a second time.

Red Flag # 8– I am Very Patient
The devil is very patient. Some men will pursue you for months or years until they get what they want. Men who scheme very patient. Delilah was very persistent. She kept asking Samson the same question, day and night. Some men will talk to you every night for 2 to 3 weeks or 2 to 3 months. People whom the enemy sends into your life are very patient. So they will do whatever it takes to get you to let down your guard, just to get you relaxed. They will ask you the same question in different ways day and night until you finally break.

Red Flag # 9 - If You Love Me, You'll…..
By verse 15, Delilah plays the old high school card. Remember when you were in high school and the guy wanted to sleep with you and he would say, "If you love me, you'll let me…." In the case of Samson and Delilah, the woman is the manipulator instead of the man. Delilah's exact words to Samson were, "How can you say that you love me? You do not need these three times and you have not told me where in thy great strength lieth?" (Judges 16:15). I had someone pull this line on me before and he really became angry because he wanted to know stuff about me and I wouldn't tell him. He pressured me for 2 to 3 weeks of daily and nightly conversation, but thanks be to God that my story didn't turn out like Samson's.

God will always intervene into the circumstances of those who have a heart for him. When he provides the way of escape, we must accept it or suffer the consequences of remaining in a soul tie. Thank God for his grace. So let's get back to Samson and Delilah.

Delilah played the love card and Samson fell for the trick and told her his secrets. Often times a player will tell you his secrets or make up "secrets" in the hopes that you'll be just as forthcoming. He presents himself as vulnerable to manipulate your emotions and leverage his position in your heart, but that's the mistake we often make as women. Just because he reveals his secrets (real or fictitious) and bares all of his soul, doesn't mean that we have to do the same. Remember, you have more to lose because if you believe the hype it could take you years to recover while he moves on to the next victim within hours or days.

Red Flag # 10 – Repeating Patterns
Here's another way to know you're in a soul tie. There will be patterns that repeat themselves. For instance, he doesn't just hurt your feelings one time. He does it over and over again. If embarrassment is his tool, he will embarrass you repeatedly. The other thing about soul ties is that your conscience will nag you. You won't be at peace because in your heart you know that something is wrong. Not only will your conscience nag you, but the person will nag you as well. Notice how Delilah nagged Samson day and night.

Red Flag # 11
I Will Nag You and Persist
When someone wants to wear you down, they need to melt your emotions and they will continue until they get what they want. If he has to talk to you every night for three hours, he will talk to you every night. It's almost like what a snake does to its victims. In cartoons, a snake hypnotizes its prey. It's that type of thing that goes along with a soul tie. You think he is just asking you questions, just having a conversation with you, but he is not. His conversation is usually part of a calculated plan to get what he wants.

In verse 13, Delilah continues to nag him so that she can wear him down. When you're in a soul tie, the person sent by the enemy continues with his goal. What would have been obvious a couple of months ago, is totally clouded by your sexual encounters. You don't even see the cliff that you're about to fall off. You don't see the trap that's being set for you. On three different occasions, Delilah asked Samson how she could harm him. If the man you're with has been a liability instead of an asset, you have to ask yourself some questions. Is this really the sign of a healthy relationship? Is this really what I want for the rest of my life? Do I want to play the fool for the rest of my life? Do I want to be used for the rest of my life? Do I want to be taken advantage of for the rest of my life? Do I want to be used and manipulated for the rest of my life? Do I want to be embarrassed for the rest of my life? Do I want to be confused - not knowing if I'm coming or going? Do I want to connect myself to someone who will nag me for the rest of my life? I believe I can answer all of these questions for you. The answer is, "No."

Judges 16:15-16 describes how Delilah nagged him every day without words and urged him so that his soul was vexed unto death. If you are in a relationship with someone and they are nagging you day and night, something is wrong. Why are they hounding you day and night? What's the urgency? He's going to see or talk to you later in the day anyway. Why does he need to hound you like that? He needs to hound you like that because he's up to no good. Granted, some men are ignorantly nagging you. It's just what they're used to doing. It's how they've always operated in a relationship. They are not aware that they're being used by the enemy. They're just used to being in toxic, codependent or enabling relationships. On the other hand, there are some men who systematically plot and scheme on naïve women. They know exactly what they're doing. Everyone isn't directly sent by the enemy. Some people are ignorantly used by the enemy.

Red Flag # 12 – Wears Down Your Resolve
Judges 16:16-17 says, "And it came to pass, when she pressed him daily with words, and urged him, so that his soul was vexed unto

death; That he told her all his heart, and said unto her, There hath not come a razor upon mine head; for I have been a Nazarite unto God from my mother's womb: if I be shaven, then my strength will go from me, and I shall become weak, and be like any other man."

The bible says that his soul was vexed. In other words, Delilah finally won. Delilah had finally worn Samson down. He had had enough. His attitude was, "I've had it. You have nagged me too much. I'm sick of hearing your voice and I'm just going to tell you what you want to know." That's what the enemy hopes to do. He hopes to wear down your resolve.

Maybe you're committed to a life of chastity. Maybe you have planned to be faithful to God with your body. Maybe you had sex outside of marriage, but committed your life to the Lord and you've decided that you will live a celibate lifestyle until you get married. But what the enemy wants to do is wear you down until you finally surrender until you break your vows. So by verse 17, everything takes a turn. Samson told Delilah the secret to his anointing. Here's what he told her: "There has not come razor upon my head for I have been a Nazarite unto God from my mother's wool. If I be shaven, then my strength will go from me and I shall become weak and be like any other man. It's over now." He actually told this woman the secret to his anointing. When a person shows you who they are, believe them. Delilah showed Samson three times who she really was. She asked him three times how she could harm him. She made it very clear that she was not in his corner. She didn't really love him. They had good sex together, but that's about it. If she cared for him, there is no way that she would try to kill him every opportunity that she got and yet that's what Delilah was doing. He allowed her to wear down his emotions.

And she made Samson sleep upon her knees. This is what the enemy does. When you're in a soul tie, the enemy will make you go to sleep. Toxic relationships make it seem like you're sleeping with your eyes wide open. Your physical eyes are open, but your spiritual eyes are closed. The enemy numbs you and he lulls you to sleep so that you are unaware of the mess that you're in. The Philistines paid Delilah 1100 pieces of silver (the equivalent of $704).

Delilah became even more vicious. The bible says that Delilah began to beat Samson herself and his strength left him. (Judges 16:19). Are you losing your strength? Do you find yourself tired most of the time? Could it be the relationship that you're in? Are you losing your sleep because your conscience is nagging you? Were you physically exhausted before the relationship? A soul tie will drain you of your energy. Delilah seized Samson's strength.

> "And she said the Philistines be upon you Samson. And he awoke out of his sleep and he said I will go out as at other times before and shake myself. And he did not know that the Lord had departed from him" (Judges 16:20).

Samson lost his anointing. He sacrificed his relationship with God to satisfy his flesh. What have you already loss as a result of being involved in this relationship? Have you almost loss your mind? Have you lost your emotional stability? Have you lost your finances? Have you lost money? Has your relationship eaten up your resources? Have they eaten up your time? Was it worth it? Was the company that good? Was the sex worth your relationship with the Lord?

9
Why You Chose Him

WOMEN ESPECIALLY END up in soul ties and stay in them for so many reasons. Sometimes we're unaware of the dysfunction that we've adopted. Out subconscious thoughts can dictate our behavior and decision-making. That's why it's so important to learn from others' experiences and to ask the Holy Spirit to lead and guide you into all truth. (John 16:13). People, especially us women, end up staying in relationships just because…..so much time has been invested, no one else has expressed interest or we're tired of being alone. These are poor reasons to remain in a relationship. I've described some reasons that we stay in toxic relationships.

Trees have roots. It's the root that makes a tree strong. If you want to kill a soul tie and stop repeating it, you must go to the root of the problem. What is feeding your decision-making? I've listed some reasons that people got involved in soul ties.

Comfortable With Crazy.
Some of us have become comfortable with crazy. We have settled for a less than acceptable relationship. We have settled for less than God's best. We stay with this person because we are familiar with this person. We feel that it's better to remain with the crazy I do

know than the crazy that I don't. When will you have room for the healthy relationship that God intended when crazy is taking up all of the space? We lie to ourselves and slip deeper and deeper into denial, singing the same old song. "It'll get better one of these days." We reason that it's not such a big deal that he doesn't keep his commitments. It could be a lot worse. In the meantime, you are getting worse. You're constantly disappointed, depressed, discouraged and in denial. All those words combined spell doom and gloom. You walk around with a dark cloud over your head and heart with absolutely no sunshine. It's time to become uncomfortable with crazy.

Generational. There can be so many causes for soul ties. It could be generational. It's how your mom, your grandmother and great-grandmother interacted with the opposite sex. It's what you've seen modeled so you copied the behavior. They all dated good-looking men who could never be faithful, but took "good care" of their women. They bought them anything they wanted, but you knew that you were not his one and only. That became the standard for a "successful relationship."

No Good Men Left. There are many reasons that people remain in unhealthy relationships. Some of those reasons may be rooted in fear, desperation, loneliness, self-hate, low self-esteem, hopelessness, familiarity and deception.

Fear. You date or court out of fear. That should never be your motivation. You fear that he'll date or marry someone else so you remain in an unbalanced, unfulfilling, toxic relationship. Either he feeds your fear because of his shaky character or immaturity or you are controlled by the spirit of fear because of some past betrayals or fear of the future. Maybe he has already proven himself to be untrustworthy, but you've convinced yourself that he's the best you can do. A man who cannot remain faithful during singleness or courtship will not be faithful in marriage. He needs to have wrestled with his demons. "Whatever is not of faith is sin." (Rom. 14:23).

How do you advance when you're afraid of being alone? Fear will torment you. The person who is fearful is not made perfect in love, but mature love casts out all fear (1 John 4:18). That is a great scripture to memorize. Anytime that we feel fear we need to speak that scripture. If you are born-again, you have the love of the Father on the inside. We must have a desire to want to please and satisfy Him at all times with everything in us. In other words, we need to love Him with all of our heart, all of our mind, all of our soul (Matt. 22:37). We need to become so filled with His love so that fear has no room. The more we meditate on His goodness, his love for us and kind intentions toward us, the less power that fear will have. Amen.

Some women believe the lie that there aren't enough good men to go around. As a result, they feed their fear more than they feed their faith. Jesus said, "Whatever is not of faith is sin." Worry is a sin. Faith and worry can't exist at the same time. One will overwhelm the other. Jesus also said, "When you pray, believe that you receive and you will have whatever you're praying for." God has not given you a spirit of fear, but of power, love and a sound mind. Perfect love casteth out all fear.

We are instructed to love the Lord with all of our heart. We are told to be anxious for nothing, but in everything with prayer and supplication let our requests be made known unto God and the God of peace will sanctify our hearts and minds in Christ Jesus. Much of our loneliness is rooted in the reality that we don't love the Lord with ALL of our heart. We are often lonely because we don't pursue, chase, hunger for, or thirst after the will of God for our lives.

When we choose not to live for God, it will create all kinds of problems and longings within us. The problem with those beliefs is that they are unscriptural. There is no lack in the kingdom of God. If the Lord has to bring someone over from London, he knows how to do that. Whatever is not of faith is sin. God has not given you a spirit of fear, but of power love and a sound mind. Is anything too hard for God? (Genesis 18:14; Luke 18:27) What if....? Fill in the blank with what you fear, i.e. What if he leaves me? What if he changes his mind? Fear hath torment, but perfect love casteth out ALL fear (1 John 4:18).

Anxiety... Nervousness, upset stomach and anxiety fill your waking hours concerning your relationship. The bible says tells us not to worry (Luke 112:25). Pray instead. Be honest and totally truthful with what you want the Lord to do for you. Thank him for what He has done and will do and His peace will flood your hearts and keep your mind in peace as your heart will be fixed on Him and His goodness. "Be anxious for nothing, but in everything by prayer and supplication, with thanksgiving, let your request be made known to God: and the peace of God, which surpasses all understanding, will guard your hearts and minds through Christ Jesus" (Phil. 4:6-7).

Ignoring Red Flags. There was a quiet storm headed in your direction, but the silence prevented you from sensing the impending disaster. You thought everything was normal and safe, but there were signs. There were clues that something was wrong. For instance, he always monopolized your time. He wanted all of your time. He called you every second of the day. In the beginning it was flattering. Eventually, it became annoying and draining. Nothing you needed to do got done. He became your focal point and priority. He monopolized huge chunks of your time. Why did he have so much free time anyway? You may have been busy doing the Lord's work, but he had some other problems going on like "baby mama drama" or lack of purpose. Sometimes, he did not keep his commitments. Just because someone is infatuated with your worship and prayer life, doesn't mean that you should invite them into your world. Let them be infatuated or in admiration of you, but let them do that from a distance so that you can keep your sanity. Amen. Amen. Amen.

Unaware of Repeating Patterns. You'll notice that soul ties have repeating patterns. My mother always kept my sisters and I involved and busy in extra-curricular activities. The guys who interrupted that flow normally had vast amounts of free time so they would attach themselves to my purpose and follow me to my events or wait for me to finish. Look at the pattern. I had purpose, focus and passion. They did not. Get the picture? Stop letting people usurp your valuable time. You cannot get time back except for when the Lord decides to redeem time, but you can avoid that by living life on God's terms in the first place. Save yourself from the aggravation.

Dating Your Assignment. God will send people into your life for the sole purpose of you helping them in some way. For a season, you have an assignment that you must complete concerning the person. Think about how many people that God has allowed you to help. Did you marry every person that you helped? Of course not! Yet, it can be very easy to confuse an assignment as a prospective mate. If you are a person who has a heart for broken people, you have to be careful. People who tend to be "rescuers" have very tender hearts. You'll know you're one of these people because people will freely tell you their personal business without you poking or prodding. You tend to also be a very good listener and are highly empathetic.

While you may not share, relate to or fully understand their pain or dysfunction, it is easy for you to empathize. It is easy for you to become their sounding board. If you're not careful, you will become emotionally attached and because you are such a "comfortable and safe place," the person calls you all of the time and is constantly taking up your time. The problem with this is that it can become dangerous if you don't have boundaries. You can end up in a relationship that was only supposed to be an assignment. God assigned you to that person's life for a particular season. Your job was to be a friend to them, point them to Christ or help them develop their relationship with Christ. Assignments are people that God connects you with for the purpose of helping them.

Many people married their assignments when they were only supposed to help them for a season. Assignments can also be very draining on your emotions. The person takes up far too much of your time and energy. Establish boundaries or they will make you their god. The trap is usually strengthened with flattery, comments like "You're so nice." "You're so easy to talk to." "I couldn't talk like this in my last relationship." Don't be so quick to get lost in the comments. While it is great to be thought of as a great listener, it is no fun when a person can't or will not reciprocate, when you're the one always offering a helping hand, counseling, supporting, strengthening and/or empowering. They may also say I always wanted someone I could talk to. I think I could marry you or I think I could marry someone like you. So understand that the glue that holds you two together, the thing that connects you is his dysfunction. What happens when he or you become healthy? Will he still be attracted to you? Will you still be attracted to him?

The Need to be Needed Some people have a need to be needed. There are several problems with this dysfunction. You only feel valuable if someone needs you. Your self-worth should not be measured by someone else. Your value is to be measured by your faith in God, by your relationship with the Lord Jesus Christ. Your children will grow up and not need you as much. If you only feel value when your friends and loved ones are broken, what will you do when the Lord makes them whole? Will you discard them because they don't need fixing? Will you feel intimidated because they can stand on their own two feet now? Will you become jealous when they can take you out to lunch? Will you become jealous when they begin to establish and maintain healthy friendships? Don't let your self-worth be defined by someone's dysfunction.

The second problem with this dysfunction is that you never grow as a person. The bible says that iron sharpens iron (Prov. 27:17). When all of your friends need you and you are the sharpest tool in the shed, how do you increase your edge? How do you become a better person? There is no one around you who can offer you healthy challenges so you become stagnate and stagnate water begins to stink after awhile and no one can drink from it. Third, if you needed to be needed in order to be valued, you are unhealthy. You feel good when others are broken. Think about that. That's sick, isn't it? And yet there are multitudes of people from every walk of life who live their lives like that. Get healthy. Seek God. Need Him more than you need anyone else.

Emotionally Needy. Perhaps, you are an emotionally needy person. You feel like you need someone in your life to make you happy. You must always have someone around you, in your house, shopping with you at the mall. You can't go to the movies by yourself. You don't know how to enjoy your own company. The problem is that happiness does not come from another person. So you may be excited and thrilled for the first few weeks or first couple of months or even the first year. In this scenario, you become a drain on the man because you have made him responsible for your joy or he becomes a drain on you because you have made him responsible for your happiness.

One person does their best to make the other person happy, but eventually realizes that that there is an unreasonable expectation and the relationship ends or drags on until one or both of you are extremely miserable. You can spot this trait because it will usually manifest in him not wanting to be alone, expressing the need to have you by his side or in his presence most of the time. Frequent and long extended phone conversations characterize this type of individual. He will inconvenience you to have his needs met. You say you have something to do and he wants you to stay on the phone while you're running your errand or shopping.

He begins to live life through you. Usually, they do not have a fulfilling, purpose-filled or passionate life. He may or may not have any friends either. Also, he usually has a large amount of free time.

When a man is emotionally healthy, he will enjoy your presence, but you should not become the source of his contentment. Jesus must be the primary source of satisfaction. It is risky to continue a relationship with such a person. In the beginning, it's flattering that they desire so much of your time, but as time goes on their obsession or addiction to you will become strenuous and frustrating.

If you are emotionally needy, ask the Holy Spirit to reveal why you are that way. Ask Him to heal your heart. Then, begin to build a strong relationship with the Lord. Then, ask Him to send healthy people into your life so that you can build healthy friendships. Ask the Lord to reveal why he created you. What is your purpose? Find out what you like to do and begin to do that. Do you like to write? Travel? Speak? Sing? Draw? Compose music? Evangelize? Feed the poor? What is your passion? Find that passion and pursue it. Remember, Ruth had purpose. She was fulfilling her purpose. Adam had purpose and passion. He was busy fulfilling his God-given assignment. Eve showed up and was presented to an emotionally healthy man.

Lonely or Alone? I'm tired of being by myself. I understand that statement. Maybe you can share your time with people who are less fortunate than you. You could volunteer at a homeless shelter. Visit nursing homes. Adopt a child. Loneliness by itself is not a sufficient enough reason to want to enter a relationship. If you enter a relationship with the wrong person, you will be twice as lonely. You will have your loneliness and now when you're around the person you're twice as lonely because he doesn't fulfill you. It's even worse now because you have to put on a show. You can be alone, but not be lonely.

In the beginning of Adam's journey, there was no indication that he was lonely. It was clear that he was alone, but he was not lonely. Lonely carries with it the sense of emptiness and sadness. It was only after Adam began naming the animals that he noticed there was no suitable mate for him. By then, he was deep into his purpose. In other words, Adam was very fulfilled. He was not lazy. He was not purposeless. He was not clueless about his God-ordained assignment. He was fully aware and fully involved in carrying out what God had assigned to his hands.

Much loneliness will be defeated when you begin to operate in purpose, when you begin to carry out the plans that God has for your life. Fulfillment is the opposite of loneliness. It was only after Adam was deep into purpose that God said, "It is not good for this man to be alone" (Gen. 2:18). Why did God make such a pronouncement at such a time? Adam had proven his manhood. He was alone, but not lonely. He had proven his ability to lead and to follow the instructions of the Lord. He had proven his character and integrity. He had a very personal relationship with the Lord. He was responsible. It wasn't until he had exhibited these character traits that God could send him a helper. His purpose and vision was clear and established. Now God could send someone to help him fulfill that vision. If you are lonely, could it be that you have not tapped into your purpose for living? If you are alone, could it be that God is still developing your character?

Loneliness is not a reason to be in a relationship. It is selfish and unfair to the other person. You are not in the relationship because you enjoy the person's company. You are using the person to benefit your selfish desire, which is to have someone around or near you so that you don't have to fix what's broken or lacking inside of you. That is selfish and immature. Be like Adam and become a whole person first.

You or the other person are always in a relationship because you fear being alone. I'm afraid I'll never find someone so I'll settle for a body with a pulse. So are those the qualifications? The person is breathing. He is alive and he can walk. The thought of being alone terrifies you so you go from relationship to relationship which usually leads to co-dependency and enabling. So two lonely people or two people who are afraid of being alone connect with each other and feed each other's dysfunction.

In the beginning, it seems perfect because you two are in tandem, in sync, you really seem to be made for each other, you can relate so well to each other's sickness. He's lonely and you're lonely. His dysfunction feeds your dysfunction and vice-versa, but what happens when one of you is no longer afraid of being alone? The bond is broken. What held you together was your unhealthy condition, Your bond is strong but it's based on dysfunction. The strength of your relationship is your dysfunction. Get healthy because even when the right one comes along you have to be able to enjoy your company. There will be times when people want their space, not necessarily because they're angry or moody, but healthy people need time to reflect, whether they go to a different location of the same room, a different room or take a walk and you have to be secure enough not to be threatened by their need for solitude.

Living Through Others. You are dissatisfied with your life so you vicariously live through someone else. Parents frequently exhibit this trait with their children. There were dreams that they did not accomplish so they live their lives through their children. For instance, a mom who wanted to be a beauty queen enrolls her child in beauty pageants as soon as she can walk and begins to live her dreams through her daughter. A father who wanted to be a track star lives his failed dreams through his son and makes his son miserable with excessive practice and unrealistic expectations of having to win every track meet.

In a dating or courtship scenario, you or the other person attach themselves to someone who is healthy or appears to be healthy. They have healthy friendships, hobbies, and a viable career. You or the other person hasn't done the work on him/herself so they latch onto someone else in an attempt to find fulfillment. The problem is that you are not a parasite or a leech, you are a human being. You should not be trying to live through someone else's life. That person has their own DNA and so do you. You are a unique creation. Invest in developing yourself to be who God wants you to be with the character of Christ.

You View Domination as a Godly Trait. He is rude and domineering and bosses you around every chance he gets. Your father did it and so did your grandfather. They were "good men" who paid the bills, provided big houses and fancy cars for their wives while stripping them of any value. She cleaned, cooked, and birthed the babies. He worked and paid the bills, but he never treated her as a partner in the marriage. She was more like a slave, a doormat or a child. She had little to say about any of the decisions and he rarely sought her input about family matters. He was the man and he made the decision. Godly leadership and domination are not synonyms. A man is to lead by example, be gentle and firm when he needs to be. If the man is rude, insulting and discounts your feelings. You're in for a miserable ride unless there is divine intervention. You might want to put on the brakes before you say, "I do". You might want to end the relationship before he robs you of the confidence and joy that remains in you.

Soul ties can be formed between friends. One friend is clearly dominating, controlling the other person. Everyone sees it except for the person who is being controlled. Again these are examples of non-romantic soul ties. I've been connected to ungodly soul ties through unhealthy friendships. I remember one friendship where she controlled and judged everything about me. One day I realized that this was a very unhealthy person. She was causing me to doubt my own worth. However, it has been my observation that most soul ties fall into the category of romantic or sexual relations.

This type of soul tie is devastating the lives of young people, families, communities and yes, even our culture. In middle schools and high schools across America, countless students are creating unhealthy soul ties – sleeping around, losing the battle to peer pressure and giving into it. This negative pattern of attachment tends to follow them throughout adulthood. If unchecked, such soul ties can lead to marrying the wrong person, divorcing and remarrying several times, producing children who are byproducts of divorce, and scattering a trail of broken and wounded hearts.

Unfortunately, unhealthy churches can also create soul ties in people's lives. Fear tactics are used in some churches when leadership insists that you attend every gathering. They belittle you or make you feel ashamed or guilty when you don't comply. Domineering leadership is leadership that controls, demands, manipulates, threatens, intimidates, embarrasses, or misuses their authority creates an unhealthy soul tie between the believers and the shepherd. The bible teaches us that the flock is God's heritage, not to be lorded over, but to be tended and biblically corrected (1 Pet. 5:3).

Rejection, Rebellion, Abandonment. Escapism, pain, financial compensation, sex or fame can also be some of the reasons people get involved in soul ties and choose to remain. Men or women who want to escape homosexuality use escapism. They will often try to suppress their same-sex desires by dating the opposite sex without dealing with their unnatural tendencies. It's like carrying a load and then packing more weight on your back expecting the burden to get lighter. It's illogical, but many people have done it. Others seek to escape the pain of a horrible past. They were abused by their husband or abused by their parent(s), so they dive into a relationship and remain in it although they're very miserable. They reason that the relationship will serve as a distraction from the pain that they refuse to deal with. Their solution backfires because the pain they stuffed will eventually rise to the surface and manifest when they least expect it or maybe there is money to be gained. They stay with the person because they know they will never have to worry about money or they enjoy the sexual encounters, but everything else about the person makes them disgusted. Maybe the trade-off is fame. He is well-connected and his position will make you famous.

Each of these reasons can usually be traced to feelings of rejection, rebellion, and/or abandonment. Children who were rejected in the womb, rejected by their peers in school, by their family or society will attempt to compensate for the rejection by attaching themselves to people or situations that will make them feel liked, accepted and valued.

Abandonment. Abandonment is similar to rejection, but may have different causes. For instance, a person who has faced a lot of deaths may tend to feel abandoned and become very clingy with friendships and relationships. Perhaps, they experienced the death of their best childhood friend, parent, sibling, grandmother or family pet while they were young. They may feel abandoned by everyone they loved and so they go from relationship to relationship creating more and more soul ties. They become possessive and fearful that the person will leave so they smother them with attention hoping to cause them to never leave like everyone else did.

Rebellion. A person who deals with the spirit of rebellion may have been dominated by their siblings as a child, dominated by their peers, dominated by a controlling boyfriend or friend, controlled by a domineering parent or boss, controlled by a pastor. As a result, that person has decided that they will never be controlled again. Instead, they manipulate and control others. They begin to take advantage of others' weaknesses instead. They rebel against authority and even the laws of God.

A Chief Spirit
I want you to be liberated. I want to help you tie up the strong man that has been binding you in an unhealthy relationship. For years, I was bound in soul ties – unhealthy friendships, relationships, businesses, work and ministries. There were many spirits in operation, but there was a king spirit, a dominant spirit, a strong man that was the source of my bondage. All the lesser demons fed the bigger demon, ensuring that the chief demon would continue to function. There are feeder spirits just like there are feeder fish - little fish that are fed to the big fish to ensure the big fish's survival.

Rejection is a king spirit that keeps a host of other demons in check under its leadership. Some of those feeder spirits are lust, fear, fear of abandonment, fear of loneliness, fear that your clock is ticking (so throw the clock out or get a new one that ticks according to God's timing. God gave Sarah a baby at the age of 90.) fear that no one will want you, fear that no one else will come along. But God has not given us a spirit of fear, but of power, love and a sound mind (2 Timothy 1:7).

This is not an exhaustive list. There are so many other reasons that people entertain certain relationships. At the time, maybe you were immature, uninformed, misguided, depressed, suicidal, filled with low self-esteem, wounded from past relationships, a victim of molestation or rape, addicted to alcohol or drugs, looking for a sugar daddy, using him to get over a past relationship, living out of replacement psychology (using him to replace and mask your issues) or a host of other reasons. Whatever the reason, make a decision to choose wisely. Choose not to repeat the mistakes of your past. Learn from your mistakes and step into a bright future.

10
Still Broken

Broken Pieces

Broken people break others.
Hurting people hurt others.
Healed people heal others.

IF HE'S BROKEN, he'll break you. If you're broken, you'll break him. If you're both broken, you'll break each other unless God intervenes. Entering a relationship when you know that you are full of anger, bitterness, fear and self-hate is selfish. Hating yourself is unattractive. Misery is like a heat-seeking missile seeking whom it may destroy. Don't let misery take you out. Recognize and admit your brokenness and the brokenness of anyone who enters your life. Jesus came to heal the brokenhearted and bind up their wounds (Psalm 147:3).

Unfortunately, some people look for wholeness by entering a relationship. A relationship won't necessarily fulfill you if you don't like or value yourself. It's important to face reality. What are your fears and past hurts? What demons won't you face? How can you expect anything good from inviting someone into a life of chaos and depression? Would you like it if someone invited you to their home and gestured for you to sit down on a nasty sofa? Suppose the couch is littered with pepperoni, potato chips, sour cream, spaghetti, potato salad and meat sauce. Would you want to sit on that sofa? For obvious reasons, you would look for somewhere else to sit, but there is nowhere else to recline. That's what it's like when we refuse to clear the junk from our lives. In essence, we are inviting someone to be a part of our messy lives. It's unfair and selfish. Ask the Holy Spirit to heal your heart from past pain. Some people are very suspicious, mistrusting and fearful because of past relationships. Suppose you do meet the one who is fit to be your spouse, but there is no room for him in your life. Your pain is occupying all of the seats in your heart to such an extent that you have no room for the wonderful man that God wants in your life. Clear away the clutter. Be the gift that you want to receive. Do the work now. Let God heal your heart and give you a fresh start. "For behold, I create new heavens and a new earth, and the former things shall not be remembered or come into mind" (Isaiah 65:17).

A soul tie doesn't always have to be romantic. You can have a friendship and be involved in a soul tie. Maybe your soul is connected to the other person, but it has a negative impact on your life. You could be in a soul tie with a business partner, but if the friendship or business partnership is unfruitful, it's a soul tie that will cause devastation.

Signs that a Person Is Still Broken
Self-exaltaion. The conversation revolves around them – how their day went, compliments people gave them, their life plans. They worship themselves or are completely self-absorbed. They always talk about themselves. They are not genuinely interested in you as a person. They are the center of their world and you are a spectator.

Negativity. They speak negatively about their former relationships. They speaks as if they were hurt by the person yesterday. They find it difficult to speak well of the person they were involved with. They find it very difficult to say something nice about the person. They blame the other person for everything that went wrong.

Quick Love. They "fall in love" with you right away. Several factors that elicit such a response. You are a good catch and they are genuinely attracted to your qualities. Maybe you're the perfect distraction. If they spend time with you, they can ignore their need to heal from past relationships and they can monopolize your time while they are on the rebound so that they don't have to reflect on what went wrong in their previous relationship(s). Or maybe they don't like to be alone and your presence keeps them from feeling lonely.

Something to Prove. They need to prove that they still have the ability to attract the opposite sex. It boosts their self-worth so they go about seeking a "quick fix". They reasons that if they can attract the opposite sex, then everything else will be okay. This keeps them from doing the work that is required to become a healthy person. The new relationship becomes a distraction from the work that they need to do to become healthy and whole. They quickly inform you of what a skilled lover they are. You barely know this person and that's what they share in conversation early on.

Track Record. Notice how they dealt with previous relationships. Did they leave of trail of broken hearts? A series of divorces? Children with different women? How did the relationships start? How did they end? What was the common factor in all of their relationship, i.e. they got bored so they dropped the person like a hot potato, found someone who looked better or made more money.

Just Divorced or In the Process. You may say this is an obvious sign to head in the opposite direction, but don't be so quick to assume that thought. A man can assure you that he is divorced or is in the process of divorcing. Either way that person needs time to heal. How can you benefit by involving yourself with a person who has not figured out why the first or second marriage didn't work. They're still confused, in denial, and/or in pain.

Divorce is a ripping away. One soul is separated from another. It is a violent thing, but the damage appears to be invisible. You cannot easily detect emotional and mental damage. It is expressed through a person's decisions or inability to make sane decisions, a person's instability, skewed perspective, clouded judgment. That's why God hates divorce. There is a wounding that results even if you really didn't like or love the person, married for the wrong reasons, i.e. sex, fame, desperation, fear, loneliness, money, looks, a green card. The results are the same. You joined yourself to someone and now you tore yourself from that person or vice-versa. Even if both parties agreed to the divorce, there will still be pain. What's scary is when people make a habit out of marrying and divorcing.

11
The Aftermath of Soul Ties

LET'S LOOK AT a great example of a young man who resisted temptation. Joseph encountered a seducing spirit in the form of his boss' wife. He had to run from Potiphar's wife when she tried to entice him (Gen. 39:7). Running will save your life. It will save your life, your peace, your finances, your sanity and spiritual well-being. I'm sure the package that enticement wraps itself in is attractive. It is usually very appealing, especially to our senses. He looks good or smells good, is tall and handsome, witty, charming and intelligent. Snakes are also intelligent, but should we build relationships with them? God forbid! Potiphar's wife was probably very beautiful and voluptuous and she was coming onto him very strongly. He had to run to maintain his godly character. He probably wouldn't have had to run from an unattractive woman. It would be easy to resist because there'd be no temptation, but what is the name of that spirit that comes to entice you and steal you away from your God-ordained spouse? It's a spirit of distraction and seduction.

Death Walk
When you fornicate, it's the enemy's desire that you die a spiritual, emotional, mental and physical death. The enemy will try to instigate an emotional breakdown, which is a type of mental death. A

sexually-transmitted disease can lead to physical death. You can also be killed spiritually. Your relationship with God can be tarnished and deeply impacted to the point that you don't make any spiritual progress in your walk with God. There's no deep prayer life or fellowship. World-renown ministers have committed sexual sin, which caused many people to lose respect for them. The enemy seeks to take your life in stages or all at once. They lost their reputation. They were no longer trusted or honored. The adversary comes to steal, kill and destroy (John 10:10).

Samson was consumed with lust and the enemy used Samson's misplaced focus to distract him from his assignment as a man of God. When you or I don't dwell in the secret place of the most High God (Psalm 91:1), we are exposed and susceptible to the schemes of the enemy. The enemy of our souls looks for an entry point, a way to access our mind. That's why the bible says give no place to the devil (Eph. 4:27). When the enemy found an opening in Samson's armor I can imagine him saying to himself, "Aha, Samson is exposed. Now I can kill him". The devil goes for the jugular. He wants to eliminate every trace of Samson so that his existence can become a memory.

Not only does the enemy want to kill you mentally, emotionally, and spiritually. He also wants to physically annihilate you; wipe out any trace or memory of you. Why would the adversary go through so much trouble? If the enemy can sidetrack you, then the people you are assigned to or the tasks that you were supposed to complete for the kingdom of God will not get done by you. How disappointing would it be to meet Jesus and not be able to cast crowns before his feet because you allowed yourself to be distracted?!!! The enemy used lust to minimize Samson's effectiveness. Don't be blindsided. Stop the madness before it starts. Recognize the red flags.

The Loss of the Anointing
Samson lost his anointing. That was a devastating and humiliating occurrence and I don't know if you know what that means. He lost the

power that God had given him. And anybody who's fallen into sin and has walked any time with the Lord God will tell you that the sin was not worth what they lost. The friendship was not worth what they lost. The business partnership was not worth what they lost. Lonely nights. Tears. Praying. Fasting. Memorizing scripture. Walking by faith. Denying your flesh. The suffering was costly. The anointing that you have costs you something. And along came a deceiver who reversed your progress in a matter of months or maybe even weeks. The sex was not worth what they lost.

When Adam sinned against God, it wasn't worth what he lost. Adam had a personal, up close relationship with God and walked with him in the cool of the day. He lost that. He lost his home. He became a liar. He became partners with the enemy. It wasn't worth it.

The Philistines cut Samson's hair, beat him and plucked out his eyes. Imagine the pain of having your eyes gauged out with no anesthesia, the excruciating, tormenting pain of having your eyes removed from your head. Samson had no strength and the spirit of God left him. So now he's physically and spiritually blind. If you are not careful and you continue to play with the devil, you will end up like Samson.

I'm not saying that the man of your interest will physically gauge out your eyes, but what I am saying is that you can spiritually lose your eyesight to the point where you lose everything connected to you. You lose your house, your car, your money, your dignity, your self-respect, your intimacy with the Lord. You no longer can discern right from wrong. You become numb to sin. You no longer have the wisdom of God. You no longer have the peace of God. You no longer have the power of God. You no longer have the joy of God.

Bondage
The Philistines took Samson into Gaza and bound him with fetters of brass. They chained him and made him a slave so now he's in bondage. Those chains were connected to an even stronger physical foundation to keep him from ever being free. That's the purpose of any

stronghold. The goal is to bind you to the strong man, to keep you from ever being free. A soul tie locks up and twists your soul, putting you in bondage. You are not free in your emotions. You are not free in your mind. You are not free in your will.

What does it mean to be bound in your will? When you're in a soul tie, you don't really want to go to his house, but you can't keep yourself from going. You know you shouldn't call him, but you can't stop yourself from calling him. Your soul is totally out of whack. You think about him 24 hours a day and seven days a week. That is not freedom. You can't think about anything else. You don't get anything else done because your mind is obsessed with him.

Samson was not only bound by physical chains, but his mind was chained long before the Philistines captured him. The chains of lust had wrapped around his mind, distorting his perception. Now he was grinding mill in a prison house like a common criminal. He went from being God's anointed to becoming a slave laborer. He went from fighting and defeating animals and thousands of men at one time to being defeated. How embarrassing! All because of lust and pride. He lusted after Delilah and he believed that he could sin against God and continue to work for the Lord without any consequences for his actions.

Idol Worship
In Genesis, after Adam and Eve sinned, part of the punishment was that Eve's desire would be for her husband. In other words, women have a natural desire to please their husband (Gen. 3:16) and such a desire is appreciated, respected and guarded in a godly union between a man and a woman. The problem occurs when this role is attempted to be fulfilled outside of a God-ordained relationship. The woman's natural desire for her husband-to-be becomes perverted and the man becomes the center of her universe. Married or dating, that was never the intention of God. NO person was ever intended to take God's place.

Dishonoring God
What else does a soul tie do? It brings great dishonor to God. By verse 23 of Judges 16, the Philistines began to declare that their God was greater than Samson's God. A soul tie brings great dishonor to the name of God. God said your body is the temple of the Lord (1 Corinthians 6:19). God said be holy as I am holy (1 Peter 1:16). So when you decide that you don't want to be holy and when you decide that your body is your body and you can do what you want to do with it, what happens?

The enemies of God began to laugh at Samson's God. The Philistines claimed that their god had the real power. They said that Samson's God didn't have enough power to keep him. This is where we began to go to the room of lust, addictions and repeating patterns. What is the rule? Who is the strong man? Often, the strongman is rejection or rebellion. But we'll talk more about that in later chapters. The Philistines were worshipping their false god and telling the God of the universe that we have your man, Samson and that was a feather in the enemy's cap.

Steals Your Joy
What else will a soul tie do? Verse 24 of Judges 16 gives us the answer. And when the Philistines saw that Samson was defeated, they praised their god. A soul tie will strip you of your anointing and people will start pointing and laughing. At this point Samson was unrecognizable so the ridicule among the Philistines would go something like this: "Samson was a mighty, anointed, good-looking, handsome, strong man of God, but look at him now." And the enemies of God will laugh in your face. They praised their god and said our god has delivered into our hands our enemy and the destroyer of our country slew many of us.

Causes Embarrassment
What else will a soul tie do? It will cause great embarrassment. By verse 25 of Judges 16, the Philistines are asking Samson to come and

entertain them. Come out here and make us laugh. They did not take Samson seriously. He was no longer a formidable opponent. He was no longer a noteworthy enemy. He no longer posed a threat. He was called and anointed one minute, but in the next minute he looked like a joke, but thank God for healing and restoration.

Samson had been cut down to size. He had been cut down like some of us have been. This man's supernatural power was reduced to the strength of a string bean. There were about 3,000 of God's enemies who witnessed his defeat. Prior to his defeat, Samson showed the first signs of humility and repentance. This is the first time that Samson displays genuine sorrow.

In verse 28, Samson called unto the Lord and said, "O Lord God, remember me, I pray thee and strengthen me, I pray thee, only this once, O God, that I may be at once avenged of the Philistines for my two eyes" (Judges 16:28). In other words, Samson was admitting his sin. He was confessing that he had messed up and he was asking for one more chance. That's the same type of prayer we need to offer.

If you've ever been in a soul tie or are in a soul tie, you want to ask God to give you another chance. He finally recognized that he was spiritually blind and he wanted the opportunity to see again, the opportunity to get his strength back. This is what Samson was communicating to the Lord.

Bittersweet

Samson had his final victory and he killed more people at his death than when he was alive. "So the dead which he slew at his death were more than they which he slew in his life" (Judges 16:30). Soul ties can be very deadly. You can end up dying in a number of ways – physically, spiritually, mentally, and emotionally. Samson died literally. God gave him another try, but it was never supposed to end that way. Prior to this, Samson would kill his enemies and still be alive. Samson killed his enemies, but he also died with them. You don't have to be a casualty.

Hope

You may be in a soul tie right now, but what I'm saying to you is that there is still time for you to get out. God will still make a way of escape for you if you want it. You don't have to die in your sins. You don't have to die emotionally. You don't have to have a nervous breakdown. You don't have to be rushed to the crisis unit or an insane asylum. You don't have to pop pills because the man you're dating has set your nerves on end. You don't have to sit on pins and needles because he won't allow you to be yourself. You don't have to sit on pins and needles wondering if he'll call you. You don't have to make yourself into another person or create another personality. In essence, he wants you to be someone else.

You don't have to be in a relationship with a person who is physically abusive because they have their own problems. You don't have to be verbally tormented or emotionally abused. You don't have to be manipulated or oppressed, walking around in a fog, paralyzed, unable to start or finish task. You don't have to continue to experience the absence of peace or the force of depression that comes with a soul tie.

You don't have to be controlled by your physical body. Maybe you do enjoy the sexual encounters with him, but look at all the baggage that comes with it. Look at what you pay for in order to get that. If sex is cut out of the picture, ask yourself, "What would life be like with him?" Is he emotionally abusive? Mentally abusive? verbally abusive? And worse yet, is he spiritually abusive? He could even be someone in the church – a church member or someone in leadership abusing their spiritual authority. But what I want to say to you right now is that if you have realized that you are in a soul tie, you don't have to stay in it. There is hope for you.

Side Effect from Breaking Soul Ties
The thing about a soul tie is that the aftermath is destructive. Soul ties are like hurricanes that blow through your life and leave you with broken pieces and collateral damage.

Withdrawals
Alcohol Withdrawal Delirium (AWD) is what happens to an alcoholic who suddenly stops drinking. The absence of the liquid poison causes a shock to the person's system and creates a bodily reaction usually resulting in violent shaking, a disturbed mind, fatigue, extreme seating, restlessness, stomach pain, mood changes, confusion and a host of other symptoms. You may start to experience withdrawals after you break a soul tie. You miss this person who called you so much and monopolized so much of your time and energy. When you sever the times, there is a void that is created, a certain level of loneliness and maybe even depression. Feel the pain and go through it anyway. Your heart may palpitate. You may feel extremely sad. The break-up may send shock your system, but it's okay. Go through the withdrawals. You'll live.

12
Reality Check

TOO BAD PEOPLE can't wear signs on their forehead that read, "Broken," "Just Out Of A Relationship," "Beware: I'm In Need of Healing," "Enter Into A Relationship With Me At Your Own Risk." Too bad we can't quarantine people or even quarantine ourselves. In the military, sick people go to sick bay, a room or building set aside for the treatment or accommodation of the sick, especially within a military base or on board a ship. We think that just because a person looks good or dresses well that they're emotionally healthy, but that's not necessarily the case.

The Signs On Our Foreheads
Whether you know it or not, there is an invisible sign on your forehead and there's a sign on a man's forehead also. He can read the sign on your forehead by talking to you for a few minutes. He can tell if you have high or low standards. He can tell if you're desperate or confident. He can tell if you're bitter or healed. It's not actually a sign on your forehead that men read. It's your attitude, your walk, your words and your life that sends a clear message to him. Are you sending out a signal of desperation that says, "Pick me, pick me. I have no one to love. I dress like this because I need attention, suffer from low self-esteem and will use my face and /or body to get the attention

that I want. I'll be a good time even though my soul is shattered in a million pieces."

You can also discern the same things about him. You just have to wait long enough to see what the sign says on his forehead. Does it read, "Respect me" or "Use me up until there's nothing left."

No Right To Cultivate a Tree He Didn't Decorate
He has no right to eat fruit from a tree that he did not cultivate. First of all, he is not your husband so he should not be sampling your fruit. Secondly, a godly mate will cultivate good things in your life that will automatically entitle him to eat the fruit that he cultivated. The bible says that the husbandman (the gardener) must be first partaker (2 Tim. 2:6). The godly man who has sown into your life, built you up, encouraged you, supplied your needs, and married you is entitled to the fruit of that tree and the crop of that garden. A boyfriend or fiancé does not have the right to sample your fruit no matter how much he has cultivated you. He must make the ultimate commitment and sacrifice by marrying you.

I chuckle when I see men trying to employ this technique. They want to claim rights that they have not earned. They have not sacrificed anything for you. They have not suffered long getting to know you. They have not been able to effectively minister to you emotionally, mentally or spiritually. And even when they do those things, you are not a Barbie Doll or trophy wife. His desire for your hair and make-up must never make you lose your identity. Often times, a man will detract from your spiritual growth, take your peace and yet want to dictate things about your life. He did not prune or purge the tree, but now he wants to decide how to decorate it. The devil is a liar! Don't let him play the hubby game when he has not earned that privilege. Don't give him the key to your heart yet; he hasn't earned that access. Guard your heart because it determines what you do.

That man has no right to decorate a tree that he didn't cultivate. Adam had every right to dress Eve if he wanted to because she came out of him. She was pulled out of him, but he was also her husband. He recognized who she was because he had spiritual eyes to see her. He did not try to change or dominate her. Be what you want. Don't ask God for a God-man if you have not become a God-woman.

Good For Now, But Not For Later
You selected someone based on your current needs, but what about your future needs? Will they be able to minister to you, encourage you, support you, mature and develop with you as your goals change, as your interests change? Will he be able to meet and support your spiritual development 5, 10 or 20 years from now?

Why You Should Not Marry Your Assignment Without God's Permission
First, he may need a counselor or therapist. He may even need deliverance. Let him go get the help he needs. You've heard the saying: The way you start a relationship is the way that it will end. You start off being the rescuer and that is probably the role that you will play for the duration of the courtship or marriage. Secondly, you should not be so invested in someone who is not your spouse or your intended. You're making marriage-like commitments to someone you are not married to. Third, marriage should not be grueling work. It should not be a chore or grunt work. You shouldn't feel like you have to force yourself to like this person. Fourth, marriage was never intended to be lop-sided – one person giving while another one always takes. It's supposed to be reciprocal. If you marry your assignment, you will probably be angry a lot because you'll be the one making most of the sacrifices and deposits into the person's life. In a lop-sided relationship, one person is always doing all of the giving and all of the sacrifice – beware. Some people run from marriage to marriage, from person to person. Be careful. They're usually running from themselves and a host of other issues that will drown them and you, if unchecked.

Does he love you or your gifts?
Does he love you because of your abilities? Maybe you're a good cook like his mother or grandmother. Perhaps he likes your mothering nature, but he dislikes everything else about you or maybe he likes the way you sing and minister, but he doesn't like your personality. There's a difference between someone loving you and loving your gifts. They can like, love or even adore your anointing, but dislike you as a person in terms of your personality and the core of who you are. You don't want to be tolerated. You want to be celebrated.

Also, the man who comes into your life has to be able to heal and boost your confidence while cultivating your spirit and soul. A man does not have the right to intrude, impose or move into your life as your priest and intercessor and covering if he has not earned it. Some slick words or enticing words are not the answer. He must demonstrate the character of Christ which means you have to get to know him to see if he is worthy of your time. You have to see him in different settings, see him under pressure, watch how he treats waitresses, ushers, children and the homeless – those who can do nothing for him.

He has no right to direct, guide or insist when he has cultivated nothing in your life. Examine what has been cultivated since you've known him. Have you grown spiritually? Have you increased in peace, wisdom and joy? Are you better for knowing this person? This person should add to your life, not subtract. God told Adam and Eve to be fruitful and multiply. This person is supposed to bring increase into your life.

How Did I Get Here?
He's goal-driven, handsome, tall, articulate, confident, but when you strip back the veneer you see that he is carrying bricks and if he doesn't get what he wants he will start throwing those bricks at you in the form of accusations and insults. You don't need anyone to suffocate you. It would appear at first that he's offering something

good, i.e. diamond earrings, fancy shoes, intelligent conversation, but there is a price tag that comes with that and the price tag would be this person is not whole or healed, but he's trying to buy your commitment to him.

Honey flows off his lips and he has such great swag. He can preach, teach and prophesy and share great revelations about the word of God. Or you felt sorry for him. He told you that he and his wife weren't getting along or that they were getting a divorce. And maybe that is true, but he doesn't need a relationship right now and adultery isn't a solution either. Or maybe he is a good listener. You talk and he listens for hours on end or maybe he shows you attention and affection unlike the guy you are dating.

Or maybe you are needy, have unresolved issues from your past. Or maybe your self-esteem was in the basement and he made you believe in yourself again. Or maybe you believe that you had to prove your value by being with someone, proving that you were still attractive and worth pursuing. Find out what attracted you in the first place so that you don't repeat that mistake. Understand your weaknesses. If you're not sure what attracted you to this person in the first place, ask the Lord to reveal it to you.

Before you can be conquered, the enemy must study its prey. What do you want or think you must have? The enemy will become a chameleon changing into whatever you desire to deceive your heart and mind. The enemy studied Eve and Eve did not fight him with the Word so the enemy won. A chameleon changes color to blend in with its environment. Some men do the same thing. If they discern that you like compliments, flowers and poetry, they will give you that. If you like "just because phone calls and cards," they will give you that. If you like acts of service – someone to wash your car and dump the garbage, they will do that. If you like manicures and pedicures, they will give you gift cards for a local salon. If you like fine restaurants, jewelry and clothes, they will give you that. There is nothing wrong with these things when the motive is pure and based on agape love, but when the motive is corrupt and tainted, you are being set up to be devoured, misused, abused, confused and manipulated.

Why We Keep The Lights Off
People prefer darkness over light because in darkness nothing is exposed. In darkness, you don't have to be confronted with truth. If my living room is dusty and disorganized, I can hide the truth of its condition by keeping the lights off. The word of God shines light on our actual condition. It illuminates our situation, allowing for the truth to be revealed. The bible says that some people preferred darkness instead of light, but Jesus lets us know that his true disciples will embrace truth, no matter how painful it is. (John 8:31-32). This is one of the conditions of being a disciple of Jesus. We must embrace the truth even when it is uncomfortable.

Have You Changed?
"It seems like I keep attracting the same type of man." Does that statement sound familiar? Your solution is staring at you in the mirror. Sometimes we are our own worst enemy. The million dollar question is: Have you changed? Are you still looking for the same qualities that you admired when you were sixteen years old? A six-pack? A shiny car? And slick conversation? News flash: You will continue to attract the same type of man until your mind changes. If all a man needs in order to become your boyfriend is a nice car, a muscular body, and charming conversation, you have short-changed yourself. Nowhere in that list is any mention of his character, a relationship with God, how he is impacting his community, his relationship with his parents, friends and siblings. You keep getting the same type of man because you haven't changed.

If a man knows that he doesn't have to work hard to get and keep you, he will not. You send that message by your code of conduct. If he knows that you're always available, that you'll drop everything you're doing to come to his rescue, that you'll do anything to please him, that you will compromise and lower your standards, there's nothing for him to work for. Jacob worked for Rachel for 14 years. What kind of love was that? Abraham loved Sarah, (maybe a little too much). His desire to please her went so far that he allowed her to play God concerning child-bearing. I am not suggesting that a man worship a woman or vice-versa. However, I am saying that women must have a standard.

They must make it clear to any interested man that they are a woman of God. You don't have to carry a banner or stamp a sign on your forehead with that message. All you have to do is ask God to show you how to become a virtuous woman and apply what the Bible teaches. You may have to unlearn some behaviors that you unconsciously picked up from your mother, grandmother, cousins, aunties and friends. You may also need to discard worldly habits that you acquired along the way from secular movies, t.v. shows, magazines and blogs.

You may have learned to manipulate a man with seductive attire and sexual activity. Do away with that! The bible says that a man who finds a wife finds a good thing and obtains favor from the Lord (Prov. 18:22). The bible does not say, "A man who finds a loose woman finds a good thing and obtains favor from the Lord." Paul told the believers in Rome not to be conformed to this world and to be transformed by the renewing of their mind. (Rom. 12:2) This means that you and I cannot think of relationships in the same way that the world thinks of them. We cannot use the same techniques and strategies to get and keep a man.

Preparation

When Jesus encountered the woman at the well in John 4, he was prepared for his encounter with that woman. When Abraham's servant, encountered Rebecca, he was prepared for her to become betrothed to Isaac. Jacob prepared and sacrificed for Leah. Boaz was prepared for Ruth. Ahasureus was prepared for Esther.

You deserve someone who has prepared for you, who has sought the Lord who has wrestled like Jacob with their issues, who has come face to face with their own struggles, and gross humanity, weakness, frailties and idiosyncrasies. You deserve someone who has taken the time to get to know, like and understand themselves. You deserve someone who has sincerely repented for his sin.

You deserve someone who will recognize, celebrate and cultivate the beauty in you. You deserve someone who will love you unconditionally as Christ loved the church. You deserve a love like that. Don't settle for less.

You don't want a half-baked cake nor should you offer such an insult to someone else. A man of God deserves a woman who has faced, acknowledged and confessed her issues and insecurities to the Father, a woman who has worked to do the best that she can with her spiritual walk, health, physical body, finances and relationships with family and friends. A man of God deserves a woman who has done her best with her career, education, the way she dresses and maintains her home. He deserves a woman who will offer him the best that she has.

When two such people unite, it will be an awesome experience. The two will become one and they will enhance each other. You two should be best friends. He should be able to make love to your mind. In other words, he should turn you on way before the marriage bed. Your conversations should be extremely enjoyable. You should genuinely enjoy each other's presence. Even when your hair or make-up is imperfect and he needs a haircut or shave, the love between the two of you should be so unconditional that you don't hold it against them even on their bad days. There has to be something that unites you beyond physical attraction.

Promises had already been spoken over Isaac when he was in the loins of Abraham, just as Levi was when Abraham paid tithes to Melchisedec (Heb. 7:10) What you do before you marry is important. You are birthing and establishing legacies in the spirit realm.

We must prepare ourselves for what we say we want. If you want a man of God, then you must be a woman of God, not in word only. Your connection to God is not solely determined by your church attendance, how many Gospel songs you listen to, how many sermons you listen to or even how many of your friends are ministers. Your godliness is reflected in your daily life and proven by the choices you make. Learn to love God with all of your heart, with all of your soul and with all of your mind. Ask God to show you how to love Him.

Second, the bible says that we must love our neighbors as we love ourselves. You cannot give what you don't have. You can't give unconditional love if you don't have it first. You have to love yourself first in a God-honoring way. What does it mean to love yourself? I have to love my body as God's unique creation. I have to get rid of body-shame. Most of the models portrayed in commercials and ads have been photo shopped. Their imperfections have been edited and let's not forget about the padded bras and padded buttocks. That cannot be the standard of beauty for you and I. It's fine to eat healthy, go to the gym and work on our bodies. That's great! But the goal should never be to look like someone else. We should strive to be our best self.

Get healthy. That's God's body that you're walking around in. He said that he saw our hands, toes and body parts before we were born. Your body belongs to God (Psalm 139:16). We no longer do things that will hurt our soul. I will no longer allow things into my life that cripple my spirit or hinder my walk with the Father. My body is the temple of the Lord so I will no longer defile it by eating food and drinking beverages that cause high blood pressure or diabetes and use the excuse that it runs in my family. It runs in your family because no one will take responsibility for their lifestyle.

I will no longer think or speak negatively about myself. I will not say or think that I'm ugly, inferior, dumb or incapable of achieving goals. I will no longer beg or manipulate people to be my friend. Or maybe you are on the other end of the spectrum and you felt that the whole world always had to revolve around you. You felt that you should always be the center of attention. Part of loving yourself in a healthy, godly way is realizing that Jesus is the source of life and he is to be worshipped. You are not to worship yourself, your house, your job, your car, your children, your parents, your siblings, your gifts, your talents or abilities.

The bible says that every good gift and every perfect gift cometh down from the Father of lights with whom there is no variableness nor shadow of turning. (James 1:17). Everything that is good comes from God so He deserves the glory and the honor for anything good that is in your life. What does it mean to love others? I will no longer use my mouth to destroy others. I will no longer allow my ears to become a dumping ground.

Thirdly, you need to discover your purpose in life. Find out why God put you on this planet and pursue his plans for your life like a pitbull. I'm convinced that part of the reason people spend so much time in wrong relationships or are in relationships at the wrong time is because they don't know God, don't know, like or understand themselves, and have not discovered the reason for which they were born. There it is! That's why you keep attracting the same type of man so do something about it. It's an inside job. Get to know Jesus and let him change you from the inside-out. Once you've changed, then you'll be attracted to a Jesus-man.

13
Know Your Worth

Killing the Spirit of Rejection with God's Acceptance

I'M ALREADY ACCEPTED in the beloved (Eph. 1:6). We don't need a human being's validation. The question is, "Is that potential suitor worthy of me?" "Is he worthy of my time, adoration and prayers? Should I even reveal my heart to this person?" That's the question. I know that I'm a good thing – physically, spiritually, emotionally and financially. I know that I am special, unique and chosen. There is nothing ugly or inferior about me. The man intended for me will love me at my core, value me and treasure me as his beloved. I will not have to play second fiddle to anyone or feel like I don't measure up. I am comfortable in my beautiful skin, my beautiful body, my beautiful personality, my beautiful laugh and everything that makes me uniquely me. I will not change or compromise for anyone because I am fearfully and wonderfully made (Psalm 139:14)) and my Father God loves me. Amen. I am uniquely chosen and handcrafted by God for his purposes and for His glory (Eph. 2:10). My Father loves me. He affirms me and takes care of me. He protects me from all hurt, harm and danger. He touches me with His finger of love and calls me His beloved. Amen.

You Have Nothing To Prove
I no longer have a need to prove anything. I now know that I am accepted in the beloved (Eph. 1:6). I now know that my beautiful Savior loves me. You've been walking around like you're an ugly duckling, but you're far from that. You have to realize that you're a good catch. There's nothing inferior about you. Since Christ is living on the inside of You, glorify Him and thank Him for yourself, His marvelous creation. Hallelujah!

You want a man that you can joyfully submit to, not one that you have to submit to out of compulsion, fear or trepidation, but it will be your pleasure to your husband because he will be like Christ. He will demonstrate his unconditional love and regard for you as the vessel ordained to stand by his side in Jesus' name. Amen.

Whatever he is will be deposited in you. If he is lustful, that will be deposited into you. You will carry and give birth to what's in him. If arrogance is in him, he will plant that in you and you will carry it and wrestle with it. On the other hand, if he is kind and mature, that will be planted in you. We are carriers.

Soul ties gather fog around your mind and make it very difficult for you to think. In fact, they make you so tired that they cause paralysis. It's very difficult to act because your mind is taken over by another entity, which is the person that has become the center of your universe.

You may not look like a model, but that's not God's standard for beauty. That is no excuse to neglect yourself. Always strive to be your best self, but never try to be someone else. You will always fail at that attempt. You can only be you. Beauty fades, charm is deceitful, but a woman who feareth the Lord she shall be praised (Prov. 31). A real man of God will appreciate you for all of you, not just how you look. He will appreciate the total package.

Values and Purpose
What are your values? What are your non-negotiables? What are the things that you absolutely will not tolerate? The things you cannot

compromise on? What are your needs, wants, and interests? What is your vision for your life? What is the purpose for which you were created? Does this person compliment your purpose?

You Are Special to God
Samson was not an accident and neither are you. You are special to God. You are anointed. Anointing means equipped and graced by God to accomplish a particular task. There is a special assignment for you, something special that God wants you to accomplish. We can abort, interrupt or delay God's plans through our disobedience. The bible is full of people who decided to disobey God. Eve ate the fruit despite God's instructions. Samson's life was cut short because he allowed his flesh to control his decisions. Sarah interrupted God's plan by giving her servant girl to Abraham. I'm sure you can think of some times in your life that you disobeyed God or ignored the promptings of the Holy Spirit. What a horrible feeling!

There is a reason that you were born. You are not a mistake or an accident. The enemy wants you to waste all of your time being connected to someone who will drain the purpose and energy out of you so that you will never fully accomplish what God intended for your life. That is what the enemy had planned for Samson. He wanted him to miss the purpose for which he was born. What better way to distract you than with another person! Unfortunately, Samson lost focus on what God wanted him to do and it cost him his life and his reputation.

He was chosen by God to rescue and lead the Israelites. During the time in which he was born, the Israelites had a big problem. They suffered from repeated cycles of disobedience. As a result, God planned for Samson to save his people from being utterly destroyed. God blessed Samson with enormous physical strength. He was a powerful warrior and he led his people in many victories against enemy nations. Unfortunately, Samson had a problem that was also of epic proportions. He allowed his lust to direct his relationships with women. As a consequence, he died from one of his relationships, which was the most deadly soul tie of all with a woman named Delilah.

14
Guard Your Heart

AS WOMEN, WE tend to be more emotional than men. We tend to be led by our feelings when we should really allow the Holy Spirit to direct our decisions. We tend to do the opposite of Proverbs 3:5-6, which tells believers not to trust their own thinking and to acknowledge the wisdom and providence of God. When we ignore God's wisdom, we end up casting our pearls before swine and giving what is holy to the dogs (Matt. 7:6).

Boundaries
Draw boundaries in your life. Stop letting in the unfruitful and the treacherous, the brute beast who just comes in and tramples on your fruit. He steals, robs, attempts to kill your destiny and doesn't replenish you.

Remember, people marry to their level of emotional health. The kind of people you select to be in relationship with reflects your level of emotional health. That's why the old adage birds of a feather flock together is so appropriate. What is in you is revealed by the company that you keep, the people with whom YOU CHOOSE to associate. Stop giving people power to hurt you. Stop giving people access to the throne room, to the holies of holies, to your tenderness where they don't belong. Until or unless they prove themselves, those corridors, doors, and rooms are off-limits to them.

Guard your heart for out of if flow the issues (*of your*) life (Prov. 4:23). Italics mine for emphasis. Teach people how to treat you. Sometimes you can show them better than you can tell them. A life time is a long time to be with the wrong person. Three months or two weeks can be too long, especially if that is the time that God has earmarked or designated for development, transformation and purification in your life. Never allow anyone to block, hinder or interfere with that. So let's put some practicality to this. How do I know when people are crossing boundaries, taking me for granted?

Signs That You Have No Boundaries
He calls you when he wants or needs something and he hangs up when he pleases with no regard for your time, feelings or priorities. He doesn't ask if it will be okay if he calls you back. He never asks if he disturbed you. He assumes that you will be available so he presumptuously states, "I'll call you back. I have another call coming in." If he takes you for granted while you're dating, he'll take you for granted when you marry him.

Hide Yourself So You Can Be Found
The man of God has to be able to find you and recognize you. Adam recognized Eve. Isaac recognized Rebecca. Ahaseurus recognized Esther. I'm not referring to physical recognition, but he has to be able to locate you in the spirit. Who are you at your core? This is something that is not learned from a book. This is learned through discernment, observation and listening. Discernment is spiritual insight and wisdom given by God. The man who is pursuing you must genuinely like you and you must genuinely like him. Nothing should have to be forced or imagined. Either you like him or you don't. If you have to force the relationship or pretend that he has certain physical

attributes or spiritual qualities, you are in for a lot of suffering. Does he care enough to learn what concerns you? What bothers you? What excites you? Only then will you know and discern if this person is the will of the Lord for your life? Take your time and be anxious for nothing (Phil. 4:6). There is no need to rush. Eternity is a long time and so is marriage.

That's why it's so important to hide yourself in God. Only God could manifest Eve. In order for a man to find you, he has to be in God himself. In other words, He has to have a relationship with God and when the time is right, the Father God Himself will present Eve to the man who is ready, who can handle her with care, who has earned the right to unite with her because of his relationship with the Father. Eve was hidden in Christ. God said, "Let us make man in our own image and in our likeness." (Gen. 1:26). You want and need a man who is so in God that you are drawn out of him, not by his own flesh, force or earthly desire. The manifestation of Eve was spiritual. It was a God thing. When God knew that Adam was ready, he made Eve appear. Eve was already inside of him. In other words, Adam had room for Eve because he had done what was required of him as a mature man. He had a relationship with God. He carried out God's assignments for his daily life. He took care of the garden and named the animals. It was Adam who had to be brought to the place in his spiritual walk with God that he was ready for Eve.

Drawing Lines in the Sand
Boundaries serve as protection. They are like fences. I remember watching cartoons where the main character would draw an imaginary line with his foot and dare his enemy to step over it. If his foe, stepped over the line, something tragic would occur like an anvil falling out of the sky and landing on his head. While we don't wish anything like that to happen to a person, that is what should happen to our spiritual enemies – lust, fear, doubt, worry and frustration. We

should put those spirits on notice. If you attempt to cross the boundaries that I have established for my life, I will shut you down. I will clobber you. I will annihilate you with the word of God and boundaries that I've set to support my Christian beliefs.

Drawing a line in the sand means that you establish boundaries. If he needs a therapist or sounding board, let him find one. You are not that one. I'm sure you've heard of the psychologists who become sexually involved with their patients. It started because they did not have boundaries. They did not recognize or honor the red flags, the caution signs that screamed danger ahead. It is the same with you. You must set boundaries.

If a man is to become a fit spouse, he must go through a growth process. He must allow the Lord to heal him. You are not Jesus. Let him learn to depend on Jesus instead of depending on you to be his rescuer. If you decide to be his holy spirit, you must always function in that role. He will never learn to depend on God and to rely solely on his ability to help, heal, develop and deliver. How can he lead you if you're the one leading him? Don't be deceived into thinking that your role is something that it is not, especially if you are not married to this person. Besides, before he marries you, he must exemplify a depth of character and resilience that has the ability to bind and resist lust, frustration or aggravation. He must demonstrate leadership ability, not just talk about it.

Protect Your Space(s)
As women, we tend to be very emotional. We are typically very empathetic and sympathetic. Our intuitive nature allows us to quickly discern someone's need and because of that we must guard against exploitation. While our desires and motives are pure in that we simply want to help another individual, that individual can end up drowning, suffocating or hindering us. When a lifeguard goes to save a drowning person, they must wait until they know the person won't grab them and pull them underwater. Somehow they have to get the

person calm first. If not, there will be two deaths – the rescuer and the other person.

Don't Take People To Your Secret Places
Do not invite people into your private space or inner circles. If there are special places that you go to eat or worship or special friends that you have, don't allow that person to share in that until they have proven themselves to be worthy. Jesus only allowed certain people in his inner circle and he only took three disciples up to the mountain of transfiguration where he shared his revelations. Only share with people who have proven that they care about you. Otherwise, you create memories that you will want to erase. You will create memories, but the only thing that you will have to show for it is scar tissue, oppression and depression. Let oppression be far from you. Don't open doors that will cause your peace to scatter. I used to introduce and invite potential suitors into my inner circle before they had a chance to prove that they were worthy of such intimacy.

Don't take people to your secret places or hangouts unless you know they're in for the long haul. If they aren't marriage material, all you're doing is creating memories that you will soon have to erase. The bible says that he that dwelleth in the secret place of the most high God shall abide under the shadow of the Almighty (Psalm 91:1). The secret place represents intimacy. If the man has does not have the character of Christ and if he does not qualify as a spouse, do not allow him to enter, dwell in, tabernacle or hangout in your secret places.

Jesus asked the question, "Wilt thou be made whole?" Will you allow the Father to make you whole? Will you give the Father time to bring restoration? Time so you can discover who you are, whose you are, and who He is? If someone is always in the space where God belongs, when do you grow in God? When does maturity have a chance to manifest itself? When does truth have a chance for actualization? Never!

Women, we are like the Holy Spirit. Have you ever grieved the Holy Spirit and He so sweetly and pleasantly, softly and quietly withdrew, but when he withdrew you felt His absence? It is the same way with women. When we withdraw, the man feels it because we helpers. As a woman, you should not be continually grieved. Those are difficult relationships to endure. The Holy Spirit longs for peace and freedom as do we. Be not entangled in the yoke of bondage (Gal. 5:1). Be free in the love that God has provided so that you become all that God intended.

It is the man who must love you sacrificially. As he sacrifices, we respond to that love. It was the Father who drew us with loving kindness. A man who cannot, will not or does not sacrifice is not ready for you. Wait until he can love you unconditinally or release him so that God can mature, develop, nurture and prepare you for the man that he has for you. The man who will love you as Christ loved the church, the man who recognizes and cherishes your unique brand of beauty, who makes you his queen, but not only feel like it, but demonstrates it through his actions. It's time for demonstration, not empty words and promises.

Yes, God is love and at some point a man must demonstrate what he claims. Otherwise, it is a false claim. You don't have time to waste on the fake and falsely professing. The wine and the oil that Jesus has poured into you and on you is too precious. It is not to be squandered, misused, mishandled or abused. God has a specific purpose for you and your life. Your oil is valuable, not to be wasted, contaminated or consumed by the unworthy or the unjustifiable. Even Jesus was specific about who he let in. They were shut out – the foolish virgins (unprepared) the man who had not dressed (careless), the ones who were more concerned with the cares of this world, choking out the word, the thorns (had just purchased oxen and a field, had just got married) making all of them unfruitful.

What's in his heart? How do you know? There's an easy way to find out what's in his heart? The bible says, "Out of the abundance of the heart, the mouth speaks" (Matt. 12:34). Give him time. Let him talk. Watch his friends. You'll find out who he is. You don't want a boy in a man's body. If you want children, consider adoption. Boys will be boys and men of God will be men of God.

Practice Saying "NO"
If you are a "yes-person" or a person who has rescuer tendencies, you must now cultivate the art of saying "No." "Come on. Say it with me." "No, I can't do that" or "No, I'm unavailable." You do not have to provide a justification or an explanation. A simple "no" is sufficient. You do not have to return every phone call or text. How you start is how you will end. Why must you always drop everything you're doing? You're teaching him that you don't have any boundaries or priorities or limitations in your life. You've established a pattern that will spoil him. You're just getting to know him. It's not that you're playing a game, you're simply using wisdom. However, if you return the text, it should be short and to the point. There is no need to explain your decision. Explanations give the individual another opportunity for access to manipulate your mind, your will and your emotions. Your motive is pure, but an impure or manipulating person will try to change your thinking for their benefit. As the serpent beguiled Eve in the garden, this person will attempt to dissuade you from exercising your free will.

Distractions
Discern the season that you're in and prepare for the attack. WARNING!!!! BEWARE!!! When God begins to promote or elevate you, look for opposition and prepare a response. Many times the temptation will come in the form of seduction. Seduction will be the enemy's choice especially if you have struggled with lust or have been waiting for the Lord to send your mate. Beware. Joseph was tempted when he had been promoted to the head of Potiphar's

household. However, there are other tactics that the enemy uses to distract you.

Flattery. He speaks so smoothly. Beautiful words glide off of his tongue. He compliments everything you do, everything you wear and everything you say. You just don't want the flattery to turn into flatulence - the accumulation of gas that exits out of the rear end. You don't want to entertain flattering speech designed to manipulate you. Words spoken by a deceptive person are hot air. You can't sell, package or preserve that kind of gas. It's good for nothing. No one wants it. "By smooth talk and flattery they deceive the minds of naïve people." (Romans 16:18 – NIV). The KJV says, "For they that are such serve not our Lord Jesus Christ, but their own belly: and by good words and fair speeches deceive the t of the simple. (Romans 16:18).

The common thread that runs through seduction is the element of deception, falsehood and lies. Seduction is often accompanied with flattering speech. "For such people are not serving our Lord Christ, but their own appetites. "I urge you, brothers and sisters, to watch out for those who cause divisions and put obstacles in your way that are contrary to the teaching you have learned. Keep away from them." (Romans 16:17 NIV) The God of peace will soon crush Satan under your feet. The grace of our Lord Jesus be with you. (Rom. 16:2 - NIV) God will give us grace to do what is right. His grace will strengthen and empower us to do what is right.

Discernment
We must know if we are assigned by God to help a person and if so, for how long, and to what extent. If I am to walk through a certain season of life with this person, "How am I to be of assistance?" "Am I to listen?" "Am I to ask questions?" "Am I to pray for and with this individual?" "Am I to physically meet with this person once a week or only on the phone?" "At what point is my help in line with the answers

to these questions?" We have to ask the Holy Ghost, "Should I even enter or attempt to help this person at all?" "Is this a distraction sent from the enemy?"

"If the person is a distraction, I have to cut this person off." "God, give me your grace and your wisdom to do so." You may be asking, "How do I know if the person is a distraction?" What was God doing in your life at the point of this person's entry into your life? Was God deepening your worship, your bible study, your preaching and teaching ministry? Was God developing your character? Intensifying your purity? What was he doing? When this person entered your life, did they bring peace or confusion, joy or pain? These kinds of questions will guard against ever developing a soul tie. People should add to your life, not take away from it. Here is where it is helpful to take inventory and to self-reflect.

Notice the Patterns
What have been the patterns in your life? Have you noticed that every time God gets ready to elevate you, the enemy sends a man? Or have you noticed that every time God gets ready to elevate you, the enemy sends someone to steal from you financially, emotionally or spiritually. It's a distraction camouflaged as a genuine need. In these cases, it is not God-ordained for you to address these so-called needs. They're traps. And this is why we must ask for God's discernment, his holy help to recognize destructive patterns.

Date in Purity and with the Intention of Marriage
Date in groups. Don't put yourself in compromising situations – lights low and alone. Temptation is hard to resist in the heat of the moment. Most scars and wounds that people inherit are during dating. Dating done the wrong way results in a lot of regrets, unwanted pregnancies, diseases, depression, and nervous breakdowns. To avoid all of that, seek the Lord in your dating decisions.

Date with the intention of marriage. Dating is not like trying on a pair of shoes. When I shop for shoes, I may try on several pair before making a decision. Sometimes I decide that I don't want any of them and I go shopping another day. Your heart is not a pair of shoes. You don't allow people to come in and out of your life. That wears on your emotions and time. Don't give everyone access to your life. Be selective and discerning.

Discover Your Purpose

One of the surest ways to guard against falling into a soul tie is in knowing your purpose. Once you know your purpose you will realize that not just anyone can enter your life. You won't feel satisfied when you "settle". After you begin to pursue your purpose, passion begins to increase in your life and you want to be with someone who knows their purpose and compliment your purpose without being envious. You don't want a person who tries to live through you and has no personal goals. They will become extremely clingy and dependent upon you to make them happy.

See This Person In Different Surroundings

You need to how he responds in times of crises and disappointment. Does he throw temper tantrums when things don't go his way? Does he walk away when conflict arises? Does he curse like a sailor or hold his peace and let the Lord fight his battles? Take your time. Get to know this person in many different circles – around family, friends, at restaurants, barbecues, and as many social gatherings as possible. Notice how he does or does not interact with others.

Keep the Dirty Birds Away

In the Mark 13, demons are represented by birds. Verse 4 reads, "And when he sowed, some seeds fell by the way side, and the fowls came and devoured them up." The seed represents the word of God. It's in a bird's nature to devour seed. It's a demon's nature to destroy. The birds ate the seed on the ground. Why do the birds keep eating your seed? Because you did not hide the word in your heart. The word of God must be hidden in your heart (Ps. 119:11) so that thieves cannot break in and steal.

The seed can also represent your talent, time, gifts and abilities. Birds are those guys who waste your time. They are also very dangerous because they devour the precious resources that God has given you. They steal your time, gifts, abilities, talent, focus, and virtue if you let them. They will rob you of your youthfulness, joy, energy, money, and dreams if you're not careful. Watch out for the birds. Jesus issues a warning in Matthew 4:4.

Everyone is not entitled to be in your space. Everyone should not have that privilege and deep level of accessibility to you. The bible tells us that when we don't allow the word of God to go deeply into us, the fowls of the air will quickly come and devour that seed (Matt. 13:4). How is it possible for the birds to devour that seed? They can devour it because you did not use wisdom and plant the seed deep into the soil of your heart.

Maybe you ignored the promptings of the Holy Spirit who will lead and guide you into ALL truth (John 16:13). The seed (word of God) was exposed allowing and inviting any vulture, scavenger, scoundrel, trickster to take advantage of you. Those dirty birds will quickly swoop down and devour all of your goodness leaving you empty handed. When you look up, you discover that all of your valuable seed is gone. In this context, the seed can represent many things. It can symbolize your finances, health, emotions, time, and/or spiritual well-being. Guard your heart. (Prov. 4:23) Don't let evil spirits, evil influences or people who are demonically inspired eat your wealth. You need to be very selective about who you allow to get that close to you.

Be Unavailable
Have you ever seen a movie where people brainwash a person or gain control of their mind? Basically, they poison the person's thinking through mind control. Cults are famous for those kind of tactics. A man can't poison your mind if you're unavailable for his manipulation. In order for anyone to gain control of your mind, body and/or emotions, you have to make yourself available.

Barring kidnapping, no one can force you to be in their presence. You choose who you allow to be around you. It's like those space alien or abduction movies. The alien or foreign object needs a host (a body). It can't possess you if you don't give it the opportunity. Delilah could not have enticed Samson if he had not made himself available.

Many times we feel like we don't have a choice so we have to settle for less. That's a trick of the enemy. Don't believe that lie. Know that you have choices. God did not make you to be abused or manipulated. He said, "Be not entangled with the yoke of bondage….Stand fast in the liberty wherein Christ has made you free…" (Gal. 5:1).

A man who wants to monopolize all of your time wants to keep you enslaved, enamored and wrapped up in him so that he becomes the center of your world and eventually he coils around you like a snake and chokes the life out of you spiritually, mentally, emotionally and/or physically. Now, you're no good to yourself, your family or anyone else. Essentially, you become the walking dead. You become a zombie. Have you ever seen those movies where people get bitten by a zombie or an infected person? Their eyes become hollow, they become very pale, the blood drains from their face and they look lifeless. To stay alive, they have to feed on someone else. Well, in order for this person to maintain control of you, they continue to feed on your low self-esteem so that they can feel better about themselves. Whether the person is feeding on you subconsciously or unconsciously, whether they are aware of their life-sucking tendencies or not, it's still having a negative affect on you and you need a way of escape. Jesus is that way of escape.

15
God's Restoration

THERE'S A GAME I used to play as a child and when one of my friends was losing, she would say, "Do over." That means that she wanted to restart the game as if nothing had happened. This was very beneficial to the person who was losing. You may have lost at the game of love, but now it's time to win. The first thing you have to do is develop a relationship with the one who is the author of love - Jesus Christ. If you don't know Jesus Christ as your savior or if you're a backslider, it's time to get things right. First, ask God to forgive you of all of your sins. Tell him that you believe that Jesus Christ died on the cross for your sins, was buried and resurrected. Ask Him to come and live in your heart eternally. Then, ask our Heavenly Father to direct you to a bible-teaching and bible-living church where you can grow in the things of God.

The next thing you need to do is let Him teach you how to love yourself. Then you need to be able to display Christ's love toward others in healthy ways, i.e. volunteering at a nursing home or soup kitchen, donating clothes, reading to children, etc. Ask God to show you your purpose for being on the planet. Before you know it, you will attract a healthy person. But remember to make sure that he's not unhealthy like you were and that he's not with you for any of the reasons listed in chapter 9. Make sure he's healthy and continue to enforce the boundaries as outlined in chapter 14.

What Your Soul Really Wants and Needs
Your soul wants and needs a relationship with the creator of the universe. You will never be satisfied until that void is filled with the one who made you. Solomon realized in his search for happiness that the whole purpose of man is to glorify God (Eccles.12:13). Has your soul really been filled with enjoying God as your Heavenly Father and friend? Let's hear the conclusion of the whole matter: Fear God and keep his commandments (Eccles. 12:13). Before Eve was presented to Adam, Adam had intimacy with his Heavenly Father. Are you experiencing intimacy with the Heavenly Father? Do you have healthy friendships? Could you be filling that void with a body when what you really need is wholesome fellowship? Do you need to exercise, develop a hobby, travel, develop a stronger relationship with the Lord?

God's mercy
By Judges 16:22 Samson's hair began to grow back. That was a sign of God's mercy. When Samson's hair began to grow again that meant that his strength would return. God could have sent the Philistines to continually cut his hair so that his anointing would never return. It's time for your hair to grow back. It's time to get back into alignment with God. And if you mean business repeat this prayer with me.

Dear Lord,
   Please forgive me for my sins which have opened doors to demonic influence. I turn from, renounce, and reject every false way. I hate every false way. Please let my hair grow back, let my anointing return and be restored. Let purity govern my decisions. Please create in me a clean heart and renew a right spirit within me. When temptation comes, I will resist it in your strength. Help me to hide your Word in my heart so that I won't sin against you. Thank you. Amen.

God let Samson make a comeback. A fallen champion was restored. Many of us have fallen from grace, but the God of all grace decided to restore Samson. Samson's soul was tied up and he was partially responsible for his condition. His parents had expressed their displeasure of his choice in women. He knew that he was not supposed to intermingle with women who did not worship Yahweh, the true and living God.

You and I are no different than Samson. Many times we knew the man was no good for us. We knew the relationship was bad, but we pursued it or stayed in it anyway. Samson was unequally yoked and committing sexual sin. He allowed his flesh to dictate his actions. He was controlled by his lust for Delilah instead of God's desires. But thanks be to the God of all grace and mercy that He sees fit to give us a second chance. Thank God for second chances!

Drink from the Well of Jesus
In the Old Testament, the well was a place of provision; it was also a meeting place and a place where miracles happened. Isaac's well overflowed to the point that his neighbors became jealous and tried to stop up his wells. Jesus met the woman at the well and it was there that a miracle occurred. An angel of the Lord met Hagar at the well in the wilderness and spared her life along with her son.

Digging for the Water
Sometimes you have to dig for the water that you're looking for. "And it came to pass the same day, that Isaac's servants came, and told him concerning the well which they had digged, and said unto him, We have found water" (Gen. 26:32). The bible says if you seek Jesus with your whole heart, you will find him (Jer. 29:13).

God had already provided supply, nourishment and provision. Everything that Abraham's servants needed was in that well. Everything that the woman in John 4 needed was in the well (Jesus). Everything that Isaac needed was in the well. Even though there were jealous people around Jacob who tried to stop the wells, they could not stop up the well of living water, Jesus Christ. Jesus is THE ANOINTED ONE. There is no one greater than Him.

This man that you want to encounter should be drinking from the well of God. He should be able to nourish you as well. He should be able to wash you with the water of the Word. He should be able to give you a spiritual bath in the water that he's been drinking from. Hallelujah! Remember, wells speak of provision and supply. Are you not Abraham's daughter? Are you not Isaac's son? Why do you act as though you are orphaned? A castaway? A second thought? Why do you act as though you have no purpose? No set reason for being? You are of royal birth! Royal ancestry! The lineage of Christ!

Why do you reject Christ and his purpose for your life? He chose you. You did not choose Him (John 15:16). You are not an orphan. You are not rejected. You are a daughter of Christ. Embrace your identity in him. Rest in that. Accept that. Tell the Father thank you for choosing you. What a great heavenly Father!

You want a man of God who can find and recognize you. Adam recognized Eve. Isaac recognized Rebecca. Ahaseurus recognized Esther. I'm not referring to physical recognition. Your man of God has to be able to locate you in the spirit. Who are you at your core? This is something that is not learned from a book. This is learned through discernment, observation and listening.

Discernment is spiritual insight and wisdom given by God. The man who is pursuing you must genuinely like you and you must genuinely like him. Nothing should have to be forced or imagined. If you have to force the relationship or pretend that he has certain physical attributes or spiritual qualities, you are in for a lot of suffering. Does he care enough to learn what concerns you? What bothers you? What excites you and vice-versa? Only then will you know and discern if this person is the will of the Lord for your life? Take your time and be anxious for nothing (Phil. 4:6). There is no need to rush. Eternity is a long time and so is marriage.

The bible says that it is not good for a man to touch a woman. When a man touches a woman that is not his, he has violated scripture and the woman has violated the Word also. Her body belongs to God and so does his. God wants to express his holiness through each vessel, but how can he do that in contamination? Many people are behaving like husband and wives without God's endorsement. I don't care how right it feels. There is a way that seemeth right unto man, but the end thereof leadeth to destruction (Prov. 14:12, 16:25).

Adam spent a lot of time with God. He enjoyed the presence of God. David enjoyed the presence of God. Abraham enjoyed the presence of God. Jacob enjoyed the presence of God. Your husband-to-be must enjoy the presence of God. There must be evidence of God's stamp upon his life. His friends, his decisions, and his lifestyle must match his profession and so must yours. Shalom. Let God become your peace, your all-in-all.

Return of the Anointing
I declare to you that your anointing is returning. When Samson's hair was cut, his anointing disappeared, but God graciously allowed his hair to grow back. If you want to be free from your soul tie today, say these words with authority, "My hair is growing back." When Samson's hair was cut off, he lost his strength and his eyes. He lost his physical eyes, but when we are in a soul tie we lose our spiritual eyes. We lose our ability to see clearly. Our discernment is lost. Our spiritual eyesight shuts down or becomes extremely cloudy. Your hair is growing back in Jesus name.

Declare this. Strength is coming to me today. God's power and healing is coming to me today. I am unavailable to the enemy. Stop letting people in your space who don't belong. Ask the Lord to widen your circles. Change, increase and/or develop your friends and social networks. Stay away from broken people unless you're anointed and assigned to them. I saw an elderly lady at the laundromat and she shared that she was washing her boyfriend's clothes. That didn't even sound right. Boyfriend? The lady was very mature in age. Why are you washing his clothes? She had settled and it showed on her face and in her spirit. He had worn her down.

16
Be Free

"THE SPIRIT OF the Lord is upon me, because he hath anointed me to preach the gospel to the poor; he hath sent me to heal the brokenhearted, to preach deliverance to the captives, and recovering of sight to the blind, to set at liberty them that are bruised" (Luke 4:18)

Ready to be Healthy
If you're ready to be healthy and whole, then you're ready to move forward. The love of God will cause you to love yourself in a healthy and balanced way. We must know that God is able to do exceeding, abundantly, above all that we can ask or think according to the power that is working in us (Eph. 3:20). We must never settle for someone because we believe that no one else will want us. Since our great God divided the Red Sea (Exodus 14:21) and made man from the dust (Gen. 2:7). He has no limitations.

No Limitations
God has no limitation. He is Beer-lahai-roi, well of the Living One who sees me (Gen. 16:14, Gen. 24:62). God has no limitations except the limitations that we put on him. We must begin to take God at his word and come into agreement with his word and war a good warfare (1 Timothy 1:18) and believe what he believes, say what he says and do what he

does because he has given us power. We're to tread on serpents, scorpions, and over all of the power of the enemy (Luke 10:19). God wants to restore the years that the locusts, the cankerworm, the caterpillar and the palmerworm have eaten (Joel 2:25). Yes, we invited some of this army upon ourselves by our own disobedience. That is why it is so important in this day and time to get in alignment with the will of God.

That is why purification is so important. God wants to use us like never before, but if we are bound and controlled by the soul of another, how can we advance the kingdom of God? The reason we're miserable is because we've given parts of ourselves to people who weren't worthy of us. We gave them space in our mind. The bible instructs us to create a habitation (a dwelling place) for God (Psalm 91:9). That person should have never occupied that space in our mind. We allowed our feelings to be connected with the wrong people and we allowed our will to be dominated by others. We need healthy connections, God-ordained connections. If your relationship is characterized by pain, feelings of hopelessness, uselessness, betrayal, vindictiveness and maliciousness, then that is not love.

Today you can begin to break free from the bondage. You can get out of it. You can be free. It is not hopeless. Jesus came to set the captive free. God says that he makes a way of escape. He says that there is therefore now no temptation that has come to you but such as is common to man but God will make a way of escape (1 Cor. 10:13). Instead of spending long hours being enthralled with the object of your affection who is controlling your soul, use this time of your life to set and achieve old and new goals, recover your strength, motivation and focus. Recover all of those things that you let slip because you made a person the center of your universe.

Time is the one thing that you cannot get back except the Lord redeem the time. But if you can avoid the accumulation of scar tissue, why not?

God offers solutions. He doesn't see that you are in a dilemma and leave you there. Our heavenly father offers a way out. It's called a way of escape (1 Cor. 10:13). And I want you to take a moment and ask yourself, " Do you want a way of escape? Do you want to be free? Or would you prefer to stay in the bondage that leads to emotional, mental, physical, and or spiritual death? I pray that you choose the first option, which is to be free so that you can recover all. Because at this point you may have lost a lot of stuff. You may have lost your reputation. You may have lost your emotional stability. You may have even lost your desire to live, but I want to tell you something. There is hope and you do not have to suffer like Samson did.

Be Honest
Admit when it's not working. Don't reason that you've already invested too much time so you don't want to end it now. So you're going to invest more time in being miserable? That doesn't make sense. Or you cringe at the thought of hurting his feelings so you stay in the relationship to spare his feelings. Let's address the first issue. You know you don't like his sense of humor. You don't like his approach to everyday matters and you don't like how you feel when you're around him. When you talk on the phone there are long pauses, awkward silences and big gaps in the conversation. You don't share many of the same interests. Maybe you have invested your time and emotions, but is that a reason to continue the charade. Should you continue to pretend? It's only going to get worse. You don't like the core of who he is. You can't mold the person into what you want. You have to accept him for who he is or cut your losses and move on.

    Let's address the second excuse. You've decided to remain in the relationship because you don't want to hurt his feelings, but you are hurting him. You are allowing him to believe a lie. You have him believing that you're satisfied and fulfilled when in reality you're miserable. That's unfair. Not to mention that you're also hurting yourself. You are unfulfilled and dissatisfied. Why torture yourself? Break up with him as peacefully as possible and move on. Have the courage to say, "This isn't working for me." Use wisdom in how and where you break-up. If he is violent or has violent tendencies or is unpredictable, it may not be wise to break up with him in private. You might want to be in a public place just in case you need to flee.

Develop Yourself – Be the Best You
Work on yourself, hang out with friends, develop and increase your prayer life, read the word and continue to fellowship with other believers who are hungering and thirsting after righteousness. Feed your spirit, but don't neglect the natural. Eat right. Exercise. Drink lots of water. Get the proper amount of rest. Style your hair. Dress in a way that pleases God. Work on your attitude. Get involved in your community. Donate time at a shelter or hospital. Visit nursing homes and read or spend time with the elderly. Enrich your life. Desperation is not attractive. It is a signal that something inside of you is broken. Jesus wants to mend your broken heart (Psalm 147:3; Isaiah 61:1).

Fill the Hole In Your Soul
If there is a hole in your soul, fill it with His spirit. And be not drunk with wine wherein is excess, but be filled with the Spirit (Ephesians 5:18). Marry the right man for the right reasons. If you're still looking for someone to make you happy, someone to make you peaceful, you haven't found fulfillment in Christ yet and you haven't found your purpose. Seek the Lord.

Recognize that God has the power to break soul ties. Hebrews 4: 12 says for the word of God is quick and powerful and sharper than any two-edged sword piercing even to the dividing asunder of soul and spirit. The word of God can divide your soul from your spirit. When God breathed into Adam, the Bible says that Adam became a living soul. God breathed his spirit into Adam. Another definition for spirit is breath. Spirit is the rouha of God, the breath of God. That's both soul and spirit.

Soul can also be interpreted as breath and spirit. In other words, God can separate your breath from your breath. God can separate your emotions from the life that he put in you. How deep is that? Only God can do that. Often times, emotions will masquerade as your spirit or as the spirit of God. But God has come today to separate your emotions from your spirit. The life that God puts in you is pure and it's holy because it comes from God. When we revisit Genesis, we see that after God made Adam he breathed into Adam's nostrils and Adam became a living soul. It was the life of God that made Adam come alive. Isn't it encouraging to know that God's word can separate the issues of your life? Take heart. Be of good courage (Psalm 27:14). Help is on the way.

When you're in a soul tie, it almost seems like it's impossible to escape it. God always makes a way of escape and that's what I love about God. No matter what kind of snares we get into, if we still have breath in our body and we still have a working mind, we can get out of the situation with God's grace and mercy.

Secondly, Romans 8:28 says, "And we know that all things work together for the good of those who love God and are the called according to his purpose." Genesis 51:20 Joseph tells his brother who conspired against him how positivity will be the outcome of their betrayal. He says of his brothers, "You meant it for evil, but God meant it for good." In other words, when Joseph's brothers betrayed him they meant it for evil. When they threw him in a pit they meant it for evil. When they sold him into slavery, they meant it for evil, but God used all of his experiences for his glory. He used negative circumstances to bring about good results. He used Joseph's life to save an entire nation and preserve the posterity of his family. Even if you're in a soul tie right now, God is going to lift you up out of it and use your testimony for good.

How to Break Free

Step 1
Repentance
You have to repent of your sin. You have to turn away from sin. Most people say you have to do a 360° turn, but you really don't want to do a 360° turn. That degree of rotation means that you have turned around in a circle and you are going to continue where you left off. You want to do a 180° turn, which means you'll end up going in the opposite direction. That's an aboute-face in military terms. That is what repentance means. It means I am turning from my sin. I have godly sorrow over what I've done because my actions grieved the heart of God. I grieved the Holy Spirit. The Bible says, "And grieve not the Holy Spirit whereby you have been sealed unto the day of redemption." (Eph. 4:30)

You may ask, "Why do I need to repent? I didn't know I was getting involved in the soul tie." But now you know. Once you know better, you should do better. The Bible says that we are to have no other God before Him. Idolatry is the worship of anything or anyone other than God. Idolatry is allowing someone to take God's place. No one is to take his place. You made this man your god. You allowed him to become the center of your universe. You obeyed his every command. You surrendered your will to his will. You gave him all of your mind, all of your emotions and all of your body, but the bible says that "Thou shalt love the Lord thy with all of thy heart, all of thy mind, all of thy soul and all of thy strength" (Luke 10:7).

Making someone your god is a sin that needs to be acknowledged and repented of. You say, "Doesn't a serious relationship require that you commit yourself to the person?" Yes, but there is also something called balance and priorities. No one is to occupy a higher position in your heart than God. God is the one who is to sit on the throne of your heart. He is the Lord of Lords and the King of Kings. He alone deserves worship. We can praise other people, but worship is reserved for God. The Bible says "Thou shall have no other God before me for I am a jealous God." (Ex. 20:3-5; Ex. 34:14). God wants first place in your life so the first thing you have to do is repent for dethroning God.

If you're ready to repent, repeat these words. A word of caution: When you say these words, be sincere and mean it from your heart. God will respond.

"Father God, I acknowledge in your son, Jesus' name that I have offended you, that I have placed (name of person) in front of you and above you. I need you to forgive me of this sin. The Bible says that I should not have any other God before you and I really need you to forgive me of this sin. You can pray this prayer or one similar to it. Basically, you are asking God to forgive you for making this person an idol in your life.

Step 2
Repent of Sexual Sin
You want to ask God to forgive you of any sexual sin - real or imagined. Perhaps, you entered into sexual misconduct or you entered into sexual misconduct in your mind by using your imagination to act out lustful fantasies. Jesus said, if you look on a person to lust after them, you have committed sin. Even if you had sexual ideas in your mind, fantasies about what you want to do with this man. That's sin also. You want to ask God to forgive you for those acts.

Step 3 - Do Away with Gifts
You want to destroy, return or get rid of any gifts presented by the other person. You might think that it is weird and unnecessary or just very ridiculous. Some women might say I'm not giving up my fur, my jewelry, or my clothes, but to hold onto those possessions is to hold on to the relationship. You are holding on to the connection. I know you're saying the two are not synonymous, but check this out. When you received a gift from him that gift was a covenant. That gift was a

symbol of your agreement with that person. How deep is covenant? A covenant is a binding agreement that is only supposed to be broken through death. That's how serious covenant is; it is a permanent commitment. So when you covenant to always be with this person, to never leave their side, you have made a very serious agreement. Thankfully, the agreement can be broken. Ungodly soul ties need to be broken so that life, health and strength can replace them.

When Abraham was walking with God, you'll notice that intermittently as he traveled he set up altars to God. What were those altars for? Those altars were memorials. They were a representation of his commitment to God. They were representations of his covenant with God. They were representations of his relationship with God. To hold on to the gift is to hold on to the person. You are holding on to the unholy, ungodly covenant that you made.

In the Old Testament, men cut covenant with blood. Jesus made a covenant with us through his shed blood. Covenants are binding. They are spiritually legal contracts. A covenant is an agreement, but when you do away with the gifts what you're saying is I want to come into disagreement with the covenant that I made. I want out. So basically what you're saying is I want to break the contract. Any time you want to break a contract you need to nullify it. You may decide to his home and return the gift, but I don't recommend that. An argument can break out and you don't need that. He could try to seduce you or he could become very violent.

Suppose you go over to his house to return the gift and he begins to sweet talk (seducing spirit) you. The conversation might go something like this: "I just want to sit here and talk with you for a little while. (Then he slides closer toward you (like a serpent). He lowers his voice, leans over and whispers in your direction. He looks longingly into your eyes and tells you how good you look and how he wished you and him could be together. The next thing you know your resolve weakens and you're back where you started from - in the bed with your lustful passions stirred up again. Or the seduction might come in a different way. He might say, "Why don't we go for a walk?" He grabs your hand as you walk through the park or as you walk to get some ice cream and you lose your resolve and become entangled in your emotions. He may even suggest that you two go to his place or your place where you can continue to "talk". Another trap is, "Let's just kiss one last time so we can have closure." Or let's go on one last date so we can have closure. A seducing spirit is dangerous.

In the worst case, he may convince you to meet him and physically abuse you. When you take back your resolve, you end up taking back your will and the cycle of manipulation begins again. The cycle of control begins again. Therefore, it's important to maintain distance from the person and destroy or get rid of any gifts that the person has given you.

Step 4
Renounce Your Vows
If you've made any commitments or vows to this person, you need to renounce them. In the heat of the moment, you've made rash statements like "I will love you forever or I'll never love anyone like I love you. I'll never give myself to anyone except you. I'll never leave you. I will always be by your side." When we're in soul ties, we make hasty commitments and unreasonable vows and we need to renounce them.

The devil is the prince of the air. That means he operates through the airwaves. That's why the Bible says, "The power of life and death is in the tongue. Choose life." (Prov. 18:21; Deut. 30:19). When you open your mouth and speak words, you are sending words into the atmosphere, which means you are authorizing things to take place. Many people think they can speak lightly and it doesn't mean anything, but your words absolutely mean something. They carry power. God showed us by his example that our words are powerful. Even from the beginning God said, "Let there be light and there was light" (Gen. 1:3).

Our words have authority. I heard a man of God say that words are our servants. God told Adam and Eve that they have the same dominion. That is, the ability to speak just like him. So in essence, God gave them the same authority. There was no need to cut the grass because everything was in divine order, but if there was an instance of overgrown grass, If the grass grew tall, I wondered how Adam and Eve cut the grass. I think when the grass was too high, they would say, "Grass be cut or grass grow low." They ruled with their words. It makes sense that they could just speak a word and things would happen. They could just say, "Grass be cut and the grass would be cut. Since Adam and Eve the same dominion and the same power and the same authority. Because Adam and Eve were supposed to rule simply by their words, the bible says that God brought all the animals to Adam and Adam opened up his mouth and named the animals what they should be called. God told him to name the animals. Whatever he called them, that is what they would be called. Whatever you say is what will happen. Whatever you meditate on or come into agreement with, is what will exist.

Whose report will you believe? (Isa. 53:1). "Is anything too hard for God?"(Gen. 18:14). Jesus said it this way, "The words that I speak are spirit and life but some of you don't believe" (John 6:63). The Bible says that you shall live by the words that you speak and you shall eat the fruit thereof (Prov. 18:21). So why not speak life? You will live by your words anyway. When you spoke to him, you may have said out loud, "I will never leave you or you repeatedly thought, "I will never leave this person" or you allow the person to speak into your ear. "I'll always be by your side,' and you agreed with them. You made a verbal contract and the enemy heard it, took that word and began to make it come to pass. Just like God takes our words and He makes them come to pass. Now what you want to do is take those words back. I know you're asking, "How do I take those words back?" You take those words back by renouncing them. You can say something like this:

Father God, in the name of Jesus forgive me for the vows and commitments that I made to this person who is not producing a positive effect on my life. I renounce any rash, hasty, vows, any last-minute commitments or vows that I made to this person. I realize now that I was spiritually blind when I made these commitments. I realize now that I was acting with an unclear and cloudy mind, but now I see clearly.

Proverbs 21:23 says, "Whoso keeps his mouth and his tongue, keepeth his soul from troubles." A person who guards his word or a man who can control his tongue is stronger than a man who can run a city" (Prov. 16:32). If you've already made these hasty commitments, you can undo them. The same way that you spoke them into existence, you can undo them with your words.

Step 5
Forgiveness

Ask God to forgive you. This may be one of the hardest steps in the process. You want to forgive the person and you want to forgive yourself. For most people, the most difficult thing to do is to forgive themselves. Some people are extremely forgiving of others, but unforgiving toward themselves. You can run them over with a Mac truck and they'll forgive you. I'm exaggerating, but I think you get my point. But for some people when it comes to forgiving themselves they go into great guilt and condemnation. Some people endure years of condemnation before they forgive themselves. Carrying such a burden is unbiblical. The Bible says, "If you confess your sins, he is faithful and just to forgive you and to cleanse you of all unrighteousness" (1 John 1:19). The Scripture doesn't say if you beat yourself in the head or run into 30 brick walls 30 times a day, then you will be forgiven. There are religions that require people to torture themselves in an effort to be forgiven by the gods, but Christianity is not one of them. Jesus was tortured so that we could be forgiven without having to torture ourselves. Some people believe that they must constantly remind themselves of their past to be qualified for God's forgiveness. However that's not what the scripture says. In other words, open up your mouth, tell the truth. Admit it. Acknowledge that you did these things or thought these things and then ask for forgiveness. Once we realize we've been involved in a soul tie, we feel used and we feel foolish. Sometimes, the hardest person to forgive is yourself, but you have to forgive yourself and you have to forgive the other person because the Bible says, "If we don't forgive others, we can't be forgiven." (Matt. 6:15). In fact, there are several scriptures about forgiveness that I'd like to share. "Forgive us of our debts as we forgive our debtors" (Matt. 6:12). What you're saying to the Lord is forgive me just as I forgive other people. You're asking the Lord to forgive you in the same way that you forgive others. If you don't forgive other people their trespasses, you can't be forgiven either.

Jesus lets us know that if we don't forgive, we will be delivered over to the tormentors (Matt. 18:34). Unforgiveness causes self-inflicted wounds to your mind and emotions. It can even cause bitterness of soul, sickness or disease. We need to forgive ourselves and forgive the other person. We can't totally blame the other person. Suppose that I am at home and someone rings the doorbell. Sin lieth at the door (Gen. 4:7). The devil wants a place in your life, but don't give it to him.

I go to the door, look out of the peephole, open the door and I let the person walk inside of my home. I am responsible for that person's entrance into my house. It was not a forced entry. I put my hand on the doorknob, turned it, and invited the person in. The person is also responsible for any acts that he commits while inside of my house. Soul ties are not just one person's fault. Soul ties generally involve cooperation between two people.

It's important that you forgive yourself. Maybe you have poor judgment. Maybe you were afraid of being alone. Maybe you realized that the person does no good for you, but you can't stand the thought of being alone. Maybe you convinced yourself that half of a person is better than no person. Perhaps you noticed your biological clock was ticking and this was the best you could ever do. Maybe you thought God was running out of good men and you'd better settle for what you can get. Whatever erroneous thoughts were dominating your brain, cancel them now in Jesus' name. Forgive yourself and others. Be free! We can't turn back time so let's learn from our mistakes and move forward.

Unforgiveness is like drinking poison and hoping your enemy will die from it, but you are the one who will suffer. Forgive so that Jesus can forgive you (Matt. 6:12). Forgive so that you won't be handed over to the tormentors (Matt. 18:34).

Step 6
Renounce the Soul Tie
You can pray something like this:

Father God, in the name of Jesus I renounce this ungodly soul tie between me and (the person's name). I now break and sever this ungodly soul tie between me and (the person's name). I know you may be wondering why do you have to say it out loud. You may be saying to yourself, "Here she goes again with this say it out loud stuff."

Here's why you need to say it out loud. It's very important that you reverse what you already put into the atmosphere. You've been speaking this negativity repeatedly and thinking it repeatedly with phrases like I'll never leave you. You're the one for me. I'll always be by your side. And all of that is negative and untrue because you're finding out right now that this is not the person who is blessing you, but rather this is the person who was derailing you from your God-ordained path.

Renouncing an oath is like using an eraser. When you write with a pencil and you realize that you made a mistake, what do you do? You erase the mistake. When you're writing with a pen and you realize that you made a mistake, what do you do? You cross it out or get some wite-out. In other words, you need to correct what was already done.

You are correcting the mistake by confessing the positive. You are confessing the truth. You then declare what God wants for your life. You need to embrace what God has ordained for your life. That's why is important for you to confess it out of your mouth because everything that God did came from His mouth. Before God moves, before God does anything, he speaks. And then it happens. It's important that you speak.

And I want you to remember this one last thing. I want you to hide this thought in your heart. Trust me. The enemy will attempt to steal all of this from you, but you are not going to let that happen. The next time that you feel tempted to let someone control your emotions, your thought life, or entire being, here's what I want you to declare. You don't have to say it to the person, but in your heart, in your mind, and out loud whenever you get a chance, say, "I will not be mastered by anyone or anything (1 Cor. 6:12). I will not be mastered by anyone other than the Lord Jesus Christ." Hallelujah! Amen.

Step 7 – Ask God to break and cut the soul ties.
When you joined your soul to another person in a relationship outside of marriage, you made a covenant with them as if you were married. It takes the power of the Lord Jesus Christ to break the covenant. You made a spiritual contract against God's will and now it takes God to break it.

The man who is for you will be sensitive to how God made you. He will have the key to unlock the door of your heart without manipulation, intimidation, coercion, force or deception. His love will be pure, tested, ordained, permitted, endorsed and sought after by God for you on your behalf. Trust God no matter what. Trust that He has an excellent plan for your life that is unfolding right now as you stay in His presence, seeking His will for your life. Hallelujah and Amen.

How do you know when a person is taking advantage of you, taking you for granted, making assumptions or immature? When he calls you, does he ask you if you're busy? Does he plunge right into conversation? Does he ever ask you how you're doing? Does he spill his guts and when another call comes in or when he's finished dumping, does he announce, "I'll call you back"? Or does he ask if you will be available to speak later or does he assume that you're doing nothing and you'll be available when he calls? Do you give him that impression? Do you drop everything you're doing every time he calls? Do they understand that your time is valuable? That you are valuable? Does he respect you? Does he respect your time? Even God doesn't force Himself on us.

"For this purpose he son of God was manifested, that He might destroy the works of the devil" (1 John 3:8).

Summary of the Features of a Soul Tie

Embarrassment – When you're around this person, you feel humiliated, awkward and/or inferior. You may even feel embarrassed about your own personality, body structure or facial appearance. In essence, he makes you feel ashamed of yourself.

A Sense Of Loss
You've loss your focus, strength, energy, determination, motivation, and appetite. It's difficult to concentrate on or complete day-to-day activities. Mental fatigue and brain fog, exhaustion are common for you. It becomes increasingly difficult to concentrate on any task for a sustained amount of time. It seems like something zapped all of your energy. You have an increase in tiredness and weariness. You are obsessed with the person's physical appearance and their body. Your body craves physical interaction with this person. You fantasize and focus on that quite often, quite frequently until it becomes a distraction and a craving that you need to frequently satisfy. You become obsessed with the person in sexual ways.

You've loss your will and ability to say, "No." You call the person excessively and you know you shouldn't be on the phone for hours at a time, but you do it anyway. It's as if you have no power to resist, no power to say, "No." You go to the person's home more than you should. You lack self-control. There is no balance. This person is has literally become the center of your world.

Spiritual Blindness - You can't see that you're spiraling downward. You're not even aware that you're being manipulated. You definitely can't see how the enemy is using your vulnerability to his advantage. Your weakness has become a playing field for the enemy and a stronghold in your life.

Compromise – You are doing and saying things that go against your values. Being around this person means compromising your integrity and your moral status. You violate your own conscience to please this person.

Lack Of Peace - You lay down to sleep, but your conscious doesn't allow you to sleep. There is a nagging at your conscience that inhibits your ability to rest.

You are disrespected. He says he will call or show up at a certain time, but he doesn't keep his word. He makes excuses to justify his behavior. He doesn't apologize at all and continues to show disrespect. He may even insult the way you dress or make fun of your personality or value system.

Your dignity is violated. He embarrasses you about things you can't control, things like your bone structure, height, skin color or facial features.

Your reasoning ability is blocked. You know you shouldn't go to his house, but you go anyway. You know you shouldn't spend so much time on the phone, but you do it anyway and important things like paying bills, grocery shopping and household chores don't get done. Your thinking is muddled and cloudy. All you can seem to think about is him and nothing else. It's like you're in a brain fog.

You're restless and your sleep is erratic. There is a general lack of peace. Your conscience nags at your soul.

When you're around him you feel inferior or confused. When you're around him, your esteem drops to the basement. You are never feel fully accepted by this person. Your flaws are emphasized or blown out of proportion. He may even dry to redo your wardrobe, make-up, jewelry and other accessories. He seems to like parts of you. He may not like your laugh and may even ask you, "Why do you laugh like that?" You may have a hearty laugh to which he may comment,

"It wasn't that funny." On the other hand, he may love your smile. He may like your personality but dislike your body structure or vice-versa. He may even attempt to mold you into the person that he desires with no regard or appreciation for your individuality. In essence, you become his project or Barbie doll. He may even try to remake everything about you.

Appendix

My Pledge

I PURPOSE TO guard my treasures. My mind, my will, my emotions, my body, my soul belongs to God. I am very valuable to my heavenly Father. He wants me to be led by the Holy Ghost, not by my emotions, my past, my lust, or my desires. I purpose to purify my soul this day. As the Scripture says, he that hath this hope in himself purifies himself even as he is pure (1 John 3:3). I promise to recognize red flags and not ignore them or pretend that they don't exist.

Bonus
20 Dating Questions

If he never changes, would you still be satisfied with him?

Do you like his character traits?

Does he love you unconditionally? Is he interested in you as a person even on days when you may not look or feel your best?

Do you trust him?

Do you trust his decisions?

Does he keep his word?

Does he lie to you?

Does he accept you for who you are or is he trying to change you?

Would you be able to love him if he were in an body or life-altering accident?

Does he treat you like a queen? Is there any doubt in your mind that you're number one or do you feel like you're in competition with his female friends, sister, mother and/or former girlfriends?

Does he apologize when he makes a mistake?

Is he concerned about your well-being?

Is he interested in your life goals?

Is he willing to sacrifice for you?

Does he share his money, time and thoughts?

How does he handle stress, pressure, crises, disappointment? Does he flee, give up, throw temper tantrums or "endure hardness like a good soldier"?

How does he treat waiters, children, clerks, taxi drivers…etc.?

Is he easily angered or offended?

Can you talk through problems with him or does he pretend or ignore your concerns?

Does he think he's always right?

Prayer for Renouncing Soul Ties
"Father God, in the name of Jesus forgive me for the vows and commitments that I made to this person who is not producing a positive effect on my life. I renounce any rash, hasty, vows, any last-minute commitments or vows that I made to this person. I realize now that I was spiritually blind when I made these commitments. I realize now that I was acting with an unclear mind, with a cloudy mind, but now I see clearly.

Prayer of Faith
Heavenly Father, I thank you for the man that you have for me, that our union was ordained by you and will be pleasing to you, fulfilling to us, make you smile and produce much fruit for the kingdom. I thank you that our marriage will be filled with Your love, joy, peace, wisdom, grace, passion, commitment, understanding, patience and self-control in Jesus' name. Amen.

Prayers for Forgiveness
Dear Lord,
   Please forgive me for my sins which have opened doors to demonic influence. I turn from, renounce, and reject every false way. I hate every false way. Now Lord please let my hair grow back, let my anointing return and be restored. Let purity govern my decisions. Please create in me a clean heart and renew a right spirit within me. When temptation comes, I will resist it in your strength. Help me to hide your Word in my heart so that I won't sin against you. Thank you. Amen.

Father God, in the name of Jesus forgive me for the vows and commitments that I made to this person who is not producing a positive effect on my life. I renounce any rash, hasty, vows, any last-minute commitments or vows that I made to this person. I realize now that I was spiritually blind when I made these commitments. I realize now that I was acting with an unclear and cloudy mind, but now I see clearly.

Prayer of Salvation
Dear Lord,
Please forgive me for all of my sins. I recognize my need for a Savior. I believe you're your blood is powerful enough to wash away my sins. I believe that you died for me on the cross, that you were buried and resurrected. I would also like you to come and live in my heart. Please direct me to bible-believing, bible-reading and bible-living church or ministry where I can grow and learn more about your kingdom.
In Jesus name,
Amen.

AFFIRMATION
I know that I'm a good thing – physically, spiritually, emotionally and financially. I know that I am special, unique and chosen. There is nothing ugly or inferior about me. The man intended for me will love me at my core, value me and treasure me as his beloved. I will not have to play second fiddle to anyone or feel like I don't measure up. I am comfortable in my beautiful skin, my beautiful body, my beautiful personality, my beautiful laugh and everything that makes me uniquely me. I will not compromise my values for anyone. I am fearfully and wonderfully made (Psalm 139:14) and my Father God loves me. I am uniquely chosen and handcrafted by God for his purposes and for His glory (Eph. 2:10). My heavenly Father loves me and He affirms me and He takes care of me and He protects me from all hurt, harm

and danger. He touches me with His finger of love and calls me His beloved. Amen.

Self-Inventory

Who are you?

What is your God-given purpose?

How does the man fit/not fit into God's purpose for your life?

What are your non-negotiables (deal breakers) in a relationship?

What are your values?

What do you need from a man?

What do you want from a man?

What are your interests? Needs?

Your vision for your life? The purpose for which you were created?

Self-Reflection

What made you attracted to the man you are currently dating? What drew you to the last man you dated?

What positive and negative characteristics did you discover in him as the relationship progressed?

What mistakes do you think you made in your past relationship(s)?

What attracts you to a man? Do you tend to be attracted to the same quality or characteristic?

How many failed relationships have you had and what do you think was the cause?

Did any of your family and friends try to warn you about any of your relationships?

What were some of the red flags that you noticed as you reflect on your past relationships?

What lessons have you learned from your relationships?

Albert Einstein said, "Insanity is doing the same thing over and over again and expecting a different result."

What behavior, attitude or character trait do you continue to exhibit over and over again expecting a different result?

Behavior is a choice. What are you choosing to do that results in negative consequences for you? What thoughts precede your actions or responses?

Made in the USA
Middletown, DE
13 January 2022